Slaves, Serfs, and Workers

Labor under the Law

by

Christopher E.S. Warburton

DORRANCE PUBLISHING CO., INC.
PITTSBURGH, PENNSYLVANIA 15222

ISBN # 0-8059-4295-5
Library of Congress Catalog Number 97-095315
Printed in the United States of America

First Printing

For information or to order additional books, please write:
Dorrance Publishing Co., Inc.
643 Smithfield Street
Pittsburgh, Pennsylvania 15222
U.S.A.

Dedication

For Henry Schwalbenberg and Magnus Macauley

Contents

Preface

I deal with a very controversial issue in this book. Not only is it controversial, it is a very topical matter that arouses curiosity, because ever so often humans try to analyze their working situations from various perspectives. We want to know, for example, why we put so many hours into our work but derive inadequate satisfaction, or why the law could not change things overnight and make us happy. Somehow as human beings, we have come to see law as the ultimate arbiter of our circumstances. It is the facilitator or the impediment to our achievement of fairness, which could arguably be defined as justice.

Justice itself is somewhat difficult to put in perspective, and humans wrestle with the concept on a daily basis. In my introduction I try to give some of the parameters that make it such a controversial issue, particularly in relation to rights. These rights are sometimes conflictive, because humans belong to societies which demand a trade-off of moral rights as against legal rights.

The historical process and the use of labor makes the entire topic of labor and law exceedingly exciting. Before the Industrial Revolution, the issue was mainly moral rights. I have presented in this book the idea that after this Revolution, various societies now struggle with balancing these rights and managing the conflict between workers and their employers in the bid to obtain economic justice. This is very difficult to do; in reality the goal is almost utopian, if not utopian. Those instincts which forced man to create societies cannot be easily subdued.

I do hope that by the challenge I have undertaken, I will generate some interests and throw some insight into the unending controversy of labor under the law.

This work is the product of relentless efforts against formidable challenges, for which I feel indebted to all those who have made it possible for me to undertake and accomplish this bold adventure. I acknowledge all those who have made it possible for me to come this far by provision of opportunity, support, and inspiration. In particular, my wife, Nabia; Dr. Schwalbenberg, an altruistic economic professor of mine; my grandparents, Mr. and Mrs. J.R. Thorpe; my mother, M.S. Warburton; my brothers, Leslie and Raymond; all my cousins, especially Benjamin; my uncle Robert and aunt Adella; Palmera Aymar; Dawn Yanek; and Peter Kelly.

I found the staff of the Fordham University Library extremely helpful, and wish to express gratitude for all the helpful leads that I was given as and when I requested them. Unqualified thanks also go to Gregory Dad-Lewis, Omotayo King, and Magnus Macauley.

Christopher Warburton

Introduction

Relevant Concepts: Rights. *Utilitarianism. Justice. The Proletarian State.*

To produce wealth or survive, the human race has organized itself into three major modes of production—slavery, serfdom and voluntary labor. These forms of organization are mainly related to economic and technological development. More often than not, they are regulated in such a way that they try to guarantee political stability.

When those who expend labor are not satisfied with the returns because of some perceived injustice, they become disgruntled and look for outlets to register their discontents. Collective rebellion breeds chaos and instability, which impinge adversely on the creation of wealth.

Wealth is provided either for the benefit of society or predominantly for individuals. Some argue that somehow society is a net beneficiary because wealth trickles down. The problem though, is that wealth does not automatically trickle down.

This work focuses on commutative and distributive justice from the time of ancient slavery to contemporary times. I will attempt to reconstruct the human perceptions of justice and what they have come to be predicated on. Though this work concerns economic relations and therefore *justice* in economic terms, the precepts on which the human sense of justice are based cannot be extricated from those which try to define the economic relations of man to man.

The fundamental mechanism for regulating all labor relations is *law*. Law is what justifies every order, redresses an iniquitous situation, or helps prevent the overturn of an oppressive situation. In law we find the articulation of ideas of men who are true to their personal convictions and who are willing to superimpose such presumptions on a wider community called *society*. They sometimes do so as if they carry around an unchallegable repository of knowledge, from which society should be ordered. Convictions are not necessarily formed without specific interests, which tend to justify convictions. These interests are sometimes rationally used to define rights in order to overwhelm others and make them conform. Slavery, which I will discuss later, was legally sustained by this mechanism. This is why law is such a powerful trajectory to espouse human conceptions about rights and to regulate society based on those conceptions.

There are two categories of rights, which occasionally conflict with one another: moral or natural rights and legal rights. Rights are used to resolve ethical or moral problems when, for example, a person is not paid after working eighteen hours a day for a whole month, or in a case where the owner of a truck company is deprived of using his property while his workers are on strike.

Natural rights are considered to be inalienable and imprescriptible because they belong to humans in their capacity as mortals. Infraction of these rights devalues the human being and alienates him from the rest of society. Recognized moral rights are normally enumerated in the entrenched clauses of some state constitutions, or affirmed by declarations, like that of the French in 1789. These rights include: freedom to life, the freedom of the owner of the truck company to own and use his property, the right to be free, and the right to resist oppression. These are believed to be God-given rights that no man or state should take away. Therefore, it will be morally wrong for a state to oppress a group of people to grow rice twenty hours a day, though the state might legally do so legitimately. The state could make a utilitarian argument that it will be beneficial to society for people to work such long hours so that society will not perish. In short, the end justifies the means, or the greatest good for the greatest number.

Legal rights are rights granted or recognized by the state or its arm(s) of government. For example, a law prohibiting the coming together of workers (call it an act of conspiracy to do otherwise) will infringe on workers' moral rights to freely associate. Ever so often moral and legal rights compete for recognition and supremacy, and humans are left with the dilemma to decide which one should be accorded primacy.

The contractarians enter the debate to argue that not all laws repudiate the moral rights of man, and that the essence of society and the state is largely to affirm those immutable, God-given moral rights to ensure the security of man. If a state violates such a contract, the leaders should be ousted by the sovereign people. The people have a rational inkling to decipher good/moral laws from bad ones. This is an argument that fits a profile of Rousseau and Paine, who are of the opinion that man entered society not to be worse off but to be secured by assurance.

Utilitarians reject the *contractarian* contention on the basis that those rights which exist irrespective of social recognition or enforcement are not entirely useful in maximizing utility. They make a basic assumption that legal rights are morally neutral, and that what should be considered is act *utilitarianism*, the act which maximizes utility irrespective of morality. The problem here is that legal attempts to expel pain and suffering cannot be explained by the same token. In other words, the moral basis catapulting such attempts cannot be ignored. Is there a moral compulsion in explaining justified legal rights?

What I have done so far is to introduce some of the basic arguments in the search for justice. I will now bring forth the relevant implications to this work. Justice is a controversial concept, the application of which depends on what analogy is being made. For example, is exploitation just if it is beneficial to society and unjust if it is not beneficial to an individual (just the kind of question the utilitarian would like to address), or is it the law that will permit this kind of bonanza that should be destroyed? What, in essence, should allow a law permitting this kind of relationship?

In *A Theory Of Justice*, John Rawls defines the concept of justice as fairness in human relations, which stems from an original position in which man ideally has a particular ignorance that will not prejudice his sense of fairness or psychological propensities. The essence of this hypothetical situation is to first ensure equality of condition for all, and second, to illuminate that when differences occur, economic inequalities should be arranged for the benefit of all. *Original position* presupposes the lack of specific interests for gain in the outcome of subsequent societal arrangement. I will consider this, the interests in the making of laws which are prejudicial enough to advantage some and disadvantage others. These laws raise moral questions.

One problem with liberal theories, including fairness as outlined, is that they scare economists and owners of property, who are concerned first with making profit and probably later with normative considerations or sacrifices that are seen as counterproductive.

The issues raise in this book concern rights, economic justice, and the state. The book is divided into two parts in order to relate (by examples) to two significant issues. In Part One I will deal with morality and positive law, whereas Part Two will deal with conflict management after the Industrial Revolution in capitalist and socialist societies.

In Part One I will argue that positive law, dealing with slavery as practiced in ancient Rome and modern America, abundantly discounted natural law, though it was known by the makers (or at least some makers) of law. This order, including serfdom in western Europe, was exploitative. I will bring out the formative years of Stoicism and its relevance to the propagation of natural law. I will further show how law legitimized this order and fought for its sustenance before the Industrial Revolution.

Although ethical problems have persisted after the Industrial Revolution, I will direct my attention to conflict management in Part Two. I will not entirely abandon these problems, but will make episodic references to them as they come up. In contemporary times, particularly in liberal democracies, arms of government have made significant strides to address the ethical issues. For example, in America, uniform commercial code permits the courts to refuse to enforce *unconscionable* contracts or clauses in contracts. C.B. Mcpherson makes the point that contract laws, which used to be the mainstay of pure market relations with no ethical

3

content, are "now, in the common-law countries, being reinterpreted to include a minimum ethical content." But it is doubtful if judicial and legislative trends are significant for commutative justice, especially because courts have difficulties in disallowing many wage contracts, except those made by unions that are as powerful as the employing corporations or state agencies. The central issue in this portion is how to deal with the notion of exploitation, wages, society, and the state.

To dispel notions of exploitation or injustice, society played an important role in medieval Europe to decide what is the just recompense. This was done by comparison on a proportional basis (i.e., comparing skills and returns of others with identical skills in society). Not only that, the cost of production and benefit to society was taken into consideration in order to reward an individual justly. With industrialization and modernization, society is much more complex and refractory these days, for which the role of the state is increasing by leaps and bounds. Some question the intrusive nature of the state. But in labor matters, I will argue that in liberal democracies, law makers and the judiciary rather than the state have spearheaded administrative functions. Has the state defaulted?

As the fundamental dispute over wages continues, and top the list of bargaining issues today, some are reminded of the revolutions of the 1840s. They clamor for the *proletarian state* as the ultimate bastion of workers' salvation to restore a sense of justice and assert rights which involve a trade-off.

The main impulse for this outcry is to undo exploitation. Marx defines this in terms of the expropriation of surplus value, for which the workers must unite to lose nothing but the chains of bondage. The labor laws that spell injustice are made by the ruling class, which has a stake in the labor arrangement. To recall my prior analysis, this will mean laws laden with interests that defy the *original position*, and outrightly epitomize injustice. But orthodox economists see things differently. They argue that because labor and capital are mere "things," they cannot be said to be exploited. Each factor is privately and voluntarily owned and receives a return equal to the value of its marginal product in a perfectly competitive market where economic profits are competed away. Yet this account fails to provide an answer for the discrepancy between actual and ideal factor payment for any of the inputs. One of the convictions of Karl Marx has not been easily dispelled.

America, Britain, and China will be arenas for analyzing the concepts of labor conflicts and how they are managed to achieve utilitarian justice. I will argue that the coalescence of interest between the judiciary and the legislature in America and Britain sometimes justify the Marxist attacks, but that the commitment of the state to the working class movement (which is an example of neo-Marxism) is equally flawed in its approach to justice. The state should be understood as an autonomous entity in domestic and foreign affairs that strives for the maximization of the welfare of workers. The use of the term *workers* in the final three chapters approximate the concept of those who labor after the Industrial Revolution, but who feel that their returns are inadequate and that unions are necessary safeguards of fairness.

Why should there be a *proletarian state*?

Marx and Engels, in *The Communist Manifesto*, contend that wage-labor does not create property for the laborer. On the contrary, it creates just the kind of property which ensures the exploitation of the laborer—capital. There is a constant clash of capital and wage-labor, partly because the capitalist exhibit personal and social status in production, and partly because the average price of wage-labor is a quantum of the means of subsistence (for example, minimum wage, which suffices to produce a bare existence). The proletarian state is therefore necessary to enrich and promote the existence of the worker.

Marxists put emphasis on surplus value. Surplus value is related to the concept of profit making. A laborer spends more time than is necessary for the production of some goods and is paid less than the value of his product.

The redundant time that is wasted prevents the laborer from producing for himself when wages are inadequate, so that he could keep on producing the goods required by the employing class. This perpetuates an adverse social division of labor. Hours of work and recompense are relevant variables to defining the concept of exploitation/injustice. A major function of the state according to Marxist theory is to prevent such adverse division of labor.

I have referred to the Chinese revolution as a neo-Marxist revolution in support of the state theory because in it, apart from other issues, the role of the peasantry is not what Marx had anticipated. Marx did to the peasants what Shakespeare had done to the plebeians. Where Shakespeare would call the commonality "curs" and "senseless things," who normally had the habit of throwing their stinking caps up, Marx perceived them as the social scum which is susceptible to reaction and decay. Of all the classes that stood face to face with the bourgeoisie, only the proletariat was the revolutionary class. The Chinese revolution challenged the contempt with which the peasantry had hitherto been held by classical Marxist theory. As always, theories and realities do not necessarily converge all the time.

Part I:

Natural v. Postitive Law

Chapter 1

The Roman Slaves

Though the Roman word for slaves, *servi*,[1] defines a benignant experience, not all slaves were captives. There were indigenous slaves, children born to slave parents, or specifically to a slave mother. In addition, destitute parents often resorted to selling their children mainly because they could not support them, but sometimes when they wanted to offset a major debt (although the law did not encourage this practice). Opportunities to change status were plentiful, and, from the earliest beginnings, the Romans practiced slavery using a few slaves as farmhands and household servants. It is highly probable that the term *servi* gained currency after the early Roman republic.[2] The number of hands needed during the early republic were few, and prisoners of war were probably killed. Later on as a rule they were sold across the Tiber, hence the phrase *trans Tiberim*. It is logical to argue by the same analogy that the great influx of slaves into Rome was the result of foreign conquest.

Roman society was hierarchical. Apart from the much more three-dimensional division into patricians, plebeians, and clients, there were slaves and freedmen with variances in privileges or recognition by law.[3] Civic duties or benefits depended on this structure, and a man's importance in this Roman society was correspondingly related to his status. In this society, we find an example of how positive law overwhelmed the natural and how an order regulated by law was made to justify a super-ordinate and subordinate relationship.

For a fuller understanding, we do not only have to look at law for its own sake but at the sources from whence it came and the spirit and intention with which it descended on the slaves. Roman slavery law, ancient as it is, is very important to understanding the vestiges in modern slavery laws.

Major Sources of Roman Slavery Law

In this section I will highlight the nature of the major sources that crystalize in the Justinian codification and how they helped perpetuate the notions of private law that regulated the Roman society. Though slaves had a moral right to be free and the makers of law were aware of this fact, no existing law espoused or admitted this right.

A fundamental premise here is that not only were the slaves excluded from the law-making process, but their interests were marginalized, and, as we shall see later, to elude this anomaly, there was an appeal to *jus gentium* in extraordinary ways.[4] The concept of natural law was first developed by early Stoics, but the terminology was coined by later (Roman) Stoics. In contravention to the theory that all laws of men are but the product of utility and convention, Stoics asserted that behind all changing laws of man is the immutable law of nature. Nature has a rational basis, and human reason is a mirror of this rationality. So that by thinking straight, man can decide not only what is right, but also what *ought* to be right. This concept of natural law is what was further developed by the Roman jurists, but was never fully applied to the institution of slavery.

Jurists

During the last two centuries of the Republic, Roman private law was mainly the work of *jurists*.[5] The jurists were private individuals with little or no ties with the government. Law-making evolved by respected opinions principally because of the neglect by government. These jurists gave opinions not only because of their talents, but also because of their social stature in the Roman society. The jurists arrogated to themselves the right to be called so. Whatever authoritative weight such opinions had was not the affirmation of the government. These men soon became heroes because a proportion of society considered their opinions authoritative. These jurists or *veteres* advised clients, magistrates, or judges.[6] By their arrogation, they did not only form opinions; they also interpreted such opinions which involved positive law and the ownership of property (slaves were considered property). They were never willing to invoke or utilize natural law for the repudiation of positive law. The character of civil law during this period was reckoned with less writing and subjected to the thoughts of learned men. They drafted legal instruments, *cavere* or *screbere*, and undertook the general conduct of litigation, *agere*.

The collapse of pontifical superintendence saw the emergence of guilded professional jurists.[7] They combined to give opinions on points of law to all who sought their advice. During the Republic, such opinions were nonauthoritative, but during the empire, notably with the seal of Augustus, the practice that jurists should give their answers by the emperors authority was active. A limited number of privileged jurists once again gained the right of giving legal opinions to all comers. It was not uncommon for the opinions of jurists to contradict each other, and the practice of authorized responsa faded out in the third century. Originally, the judge had to take account of living jurists when opinions conflicted, particularly those who enjoyed *jus respondendi* produced by the parties with regard to the matter at hand. Later this authority was also extended to dead jurists.

The Twelve Tables

The arguments for the *Tables* suggest that before its compilation, there was a particular paucity of the knowledge about positive law among those the law was intended to order. More importantly, the *Tables* was a mere affirmation of those practices to which society had been subjected.

The conditions which necessitated the *Twelve Tables* suggest that knowledge of the law was limited (to privileged groups) and its enforcement was arbitrary. The *Twelve Tables* was a product of the remonstrance of plebeians who complained that knowledge of the law was withheld from them and that its enforcement by patrician consuls was arbitrary and tyrannical. In 462 B.C. Gaius Terentilus Arsa, one of the tribunes, proposed measures of reform. It took ten years of bickering and civil upheaval to arrive at an agreement. When the commotion finally subsided, commissioners were to be appointed to draw up a code of law. Three delegates were sent to Greece to inquire into the laws of the Greek states, and particularly to peruse the code that Solon gave to Athens. After the Greek expedition, ten patricians were appointed to hold office during the ensuing year. Their prime aim was codification. From their decisions, there was to be no appeal to the people, and the functions of magistrates were to be suspended. The ten patricians—*decem viri*, otherwise called *decemvirs*—drew up ten tables of laws which were submitted to and approved by the *comitia centuriata* (451 B.C.). The work was inadequate, and a new commission of ten (this time including plebeians) was appointed for the following year. The result was two more tables, inequitable in the eyes of Cicero which were nevertheless submitted to the *comitia*. "The law of the *Twelve Tables*" was looked upon by the Romans of later ages as the starting point of their legal history. E. Levy and T. Richards call it "the fountain of all public and private law."[8] This "code" was formally in force until it was superseded by Justinian legislation almost ten centuries later. The net effect of these *Tables* was the reenactment or resonance of customary practices. The laws of the *Tables* were of an exigent variety and left untouched principles which had not been called into question. As R.W. Lee puts it, the Tables mirror "a primitive agricultural society, in which government has scarcely emerged from the stage of regulated self-help, in which law has not yet been disentagled from religion."[9] We do not know for certain the contents of these laws, but the relevant intuition here is to observe the force of customary practices and how they were held sacrosanct for the functioning of this society.

The Magistrates

Roman Magistrates fell into various categories. There were those who had *imperium*, supreme executive authority which had hitherto been vested in the king during the regal period, and those without *imperium: censor, tribune, aedile, quaestor*. The magistrates gained much prominence during the republic, owing to the expiration of the regal period. They all had *potestas*, power, which was sufficient to enforce the authority of their office.

The individual magistracies included consuls, praetors, censors, aediles, quaestors, tribunes, and dictators. As the tasks of the consuls become more elaborate, functions were transferred over to the censors, praetors, and aediles. After the dictatorship fell into disuse, the consuls were normally empowered by the Senate with dictatorial powers. The laws made by the magistrates confirm their interests, which they also interpreted for the smooth running of the society. None of these magistrates deviated from the normally perceived functions of positive law as they relate to slavery.

Praetors

Praetors took over the judicial functions of the consul, *praetor urbanus*, and oftentimes were appointed to superintend cases in which a foreigner was concerned, *praetor peregrinus*. Praetors were important for the development of positive law. They had control of courts, and issued edicts which interpreted their duties and how they would go about exercising their offices. Though the praetors were not charged with the responsibility of making laws, by granting, refuting, and limiting remedies, they facilitated legal change.[10] Edicts were tantamount to governmental law-making. There was some form of cooperation or collaboration between praetors and jurists. Though the praetor may take credit for introducing the contract of sale or partnership, the substance of such contracts was the work of jurists. Successive generations of praetors were to bring into life a supplementary body of law—*jus praetorium*, although this was not absorbed into civil law. Praetorian actions were actions for which civil law precedent was lacking.[11]

Aediles

There were *plebeian* and *curule* aediles.[12] The aediles presided over issues dealing with public buildings, policing the city, and controlling the markets. Some of the rules made by the *curule* aediles in the law of sale have even left their impression on modern societies that have inherited Roman tradition. The law contained in their edicts was known as the *jus honorarium* because it came from holders of offices (*honores*). Some of the rules associated with their office include the declaration of certain specified defects which were either moral or physical, so that sellers of slaves and cattle were obligated to make defects known to potential buyers. Whether defects were known or not, punitive impositions were made on the sellers when defects were detected. These were *actio red-hibitoria* and *quanti minoris*. Six months were given for redhibitory defects, which destroyed or impaired the utility of the good to the purchaser. For *quanti minoris*, the purchaser affirmed the sale but claimed a reduction in price. This was done within a period of a whole year.

The *Comitia* or Popular Assemblies

By the time of the Republic, there were three main citizen assemblies: *curiata, comitia centuriata,* and *comitia tributa*. Among the functions of the *comitia tributa* was the task of judicially taking cognizance of appeals in certain cases in which capital punishment was not amiss. All of these assemblies had legislative powers, although their influence diminished under the empire. Slaves could not have representation in these assemblies.

Senate Recommendations and Decrees

The senate made recommendations that had the force of law. One recommendation (A.D. 10) punished slaves for the unlawful death of their masters. The rule stipulates that if an owner of slaves was killed, all slaves within earshot at the time had to be interrogated under torture and executed. Senatorial recommendations were introduced to require the interrogation by the state of slaves of men who had been murdered. Providing insight into the senate recommendations, Labeo (one of the jurists) makes the point that whenever violence was used in a way that normally resulted in death, it had to be taken that senate recommendation would apply. The rationale behind this intimidation, according to jurists, was to make sure that no household will be unprotected. The threat of danger to the lives of slaves was an insurance policy for slaves to protect their masters against internal and external enemies.

The senate could not initiate business on its own accord. It was normally convened by the invitation of a magistrate like the quaestor, who summoned it to convocate and defined the scope of business for discussion. Discussions were held, and, when appropriate, a vote was taken. A vote of the senate when it was in proper order and was accepted was called *senatus consultum*, but if vetoed by a magistrate with the necessary authority it was *senatus auctoritas* or mere expression of opinion. The *senatus consultum* was more or less a decree by the senate. By the second century B.C., it was not uncommon for the senate to issue decrees concerning the status of slaves. One of the decrees was a cause for war, *casus belli*.

The Justinian Code

The varied and uncontrollable number of Roman laws was problematic by the time of the empire, when Justinianus Flavius Petrus Sabbatius (A.D. 483—565) became emperor of the East Roman/Byzantine Empire in 527. In A.D. 476 the West had suffered serious reverses as a result of Barbarian incursions, and the threat of collapse or decay was manifest in the administration of the Roman Empire. Justinian was determined to revive the glories of older Rome in law and empire. He was probably inspired by what the Barbarian kings were doing in the West with the compilation of law that was described as *leges Barbarorum*.[13]

It should be noticed that earlier attempts at imperial codification had been made by Thedosius II in 438. These attempts were, however, limited to edicts issued by emperors, beginning with Constantine in 312. They disregarded commentaries of jurists, as well as those edicts which were issued before that date. Justinian assigned a committee headed by his quaestor (described as "brilliant but corrupt Tribonian") the task of reading law books and millions of lines of legal works with several goals including: (i) the creation of a standard workbook or syllabus for the use of students; (ii) the collection of commentary of jurisconsults on the law; and (iii) the collection and editing of all legislation still valid.

The effort was hasty and resulted in inaccuracies in the first edition (529). The revised edition came in 534, with Justinian's own legislation postdating 529. The code was partitioned into three sections (which corresponded to the goals already identified). The first was the *Institutes*, or legal workbook; the second, the *Digest*, or commentary of jurists on the civil law beginning with the second century A.D.; and the third, imperial legislation.[14] Some forty jurists supplied the material for the digest in unequal degree: one third from Domitius Ulpianus, one half from Ulpian and E.F. Paul combined, and two-thirds from the five jurists who occupy the place of honor in the law of citations. The great majority is from the classical age of Roman jurisprudence—from the beginning of the empire to the middle of the third century. Contrary to instruction, the Compilers included a few jurists who had not been given the right to give legal opinions to all courts (*jus respondendi*). Imperial legislation was a compilation of that running from the early second century up to Justinian's own time. This tripartite composition was the collection of Justinian law known as *Corpus Juris Civilis*. To it was appended the *Novellae*, words which were statutes, necessitated mostly by exigencies (since human circumstances are dynamic). The *Novels* were an attempt to reflect current Byzantine practice, rather than pure Roman law.

Gaius is acknowledged as the main source of Justinian's *Institutes*, both in content and structure. It is argued that it was from Gaius that Justinian drew his division of the whole outline of private law under the headings of persons, things, and actions. It is particularly striking that even as editions and modifications were made, Gaius is the only classical jurist who has left behind a complete book untouched by Justinian editors. From Gaius we learn that the main classification in the law of persons is that all men were either free or slaves, and that among free men some are *freeborn* while others are *freed*. *Freeborn* are those who were born free; freedmen are those who have been manumitted from lawful slavery. In addition, there are three classes of freemen: Roman citizens, Latins, and capitulated aliens.

I have alluded to Roman law and its sources to show later how this law regulated slavery and justified that order. The Justinian compilation is the most comprehensive remnant of Roman law that has ben handed down to modern society. It facilitates our understanding of Roman legal culture, for it gives the clearest rationale behind the organization of slave society.

The Roman Slaves

In my introductory theoretical background, I laid the basis for an understanding of injustice and exploitation. I made the point that work and recompense for hourly input are very good indicators, but that in addition, there must be undue benefit to the employer class, which is able to etch such profits by calculated practices. The tendency is to reproduce and perpetuate the system. To accomplish this goal, law is the most powerful trajectory to hold one faction in submission, or at least to explain the *status quo*, thereby justifying it. I will now turn to establishing that the exploited had economic value, but that their status and rewards were, for the most part, regulated by positive law and not natural law.

Roman slavery was predicated on the idea that slavery is an institution of common law or the common law of peoples already referred to as *jus gentium*, by which a person is put into the ownership or *dominium* of somebody else. This is ironically the only law that is held contrary to the natural order. Of the three classifications in the private law—persons, things, and actions—slaves were classified as "things"(*res*). By "things," the

Romans meant things of economic value. They have economic interests guaranteed by law, so that *res* would mean things having pecuniary value which the law will protect. The law relating to things, therefore, is the law relating to property, encompassing the law of obligations and the law of succession. Things were further classified into movable and unmovable, mancipable and nonmancipable, or *res mancipi* and *res nec mancipi*. These are either in one's patrimony or outside one's patrimony. Thus, certain things are subject to private ownership, but others are not. Things which are common to all men are not subject to private ownership; these are *res communes* (for example, air, running water, and the sea). Some belong to the corporate body, *res universitas*, like theatres and race courses, and others to no one, *res nullius*; for example, churches and things dedicated to the service of God. The distinction became confused over things common and things public. As abolition of clumsy distinctions became warranted, Justinian made some deletions. Similarly, what could be movable for one purpose might not be for another. Consequently, the attitude of the law to things is striking.

Because the slaves were things subject to private ownership, they could own no property. Slaves belonging to the category of *res mancipi* represented an important class of poverty in agricultural society. As far back as the third century B.C., this class of slaves was a subject matter of contract for sale or hire with no warranty until the *curule aediles* issued edicts relating to the sale of slaves in the Roman markets. This edict protected the buyer of slaves by forewarning them (*caveat emptor*) about defects which were only pertinent to the purchase. During the republic a much more elaborate and safer edict was provided. The edict states:

> Let those who sell slaves inform the purchasers what are the diseases and defects of each, who is a runaway or given to wandering off or who is liable for noxal surrender. And when the slaves are sold, let them declare all these matters openly and correctly.[15]

The status of slaves as defined was ambivalent. Though the slave was a "thing," he was granted personality status also in law, because he was a person capable of human rights and duties. He could testify in court, albeit under extraordinary conditions, and could be charged with murder. Although this personality thesis was developed and shaped during the Byzantine period under Christian theological influence, it had always been an implicit legal anomaly. The slaves were clearly always subjects of criminal law, but the law attempted to circumvent or disregard the personality issue when it defined the status of slaves.

The deprivation of personality made it feasible for masters to derive unrestrained benefits from the slaves' restrained conditions. The reward for labor was determined by the peculium, which involved all forms of arbitrary gratis. But the concept of peculium itself was vague and ill-defined. It was subject to the vacillations of the master, who had unfettered sway over it. The creation of a peculium was an act of administration entirely within an owner's affairs. It abetted fraudulent schemes to protract slave labor, and the *Justinian Digest* typifies some of the controversies with which it was fraught. From the *Digest* we learn that a peculium was problematic on another front. If the ordinary slave of a master (*ordinarius*) had a slave of his own (*vicarius*) complications arose as to whether the master could deduct from the peculium of the *vicarius* to cover a debt owed by the *ordinarius*. However, complicating the issue was that the masters reserved the right to tamper, manipulate, or even repudiate the peculium because the peculium was never treated as delivered until it was in the hands of the slaves. The peculium, as a matter of fact, was reserved for skilled urban slaves, not for rural workers.[16]

The comfortable, the well off, and the wealthy all employed slaves as domestic servants. Roman slaves were also found in industrial and commercial pursuits. They were used for mining, since few of the freemen would condescend to countenance the deplorable conditions in the mines. Slaves were also found to be managers, accountants, shopkeepers, and secretaries.

There was increased wealth of the elite occasioned by slave labor which permitted heavy investment in land. Since senators were forbidden by law to engage in trade and manufacturing, they acquired lands in the provinces and portions of public land (*ager publicus* in Italy), which were amalgamated into large scale latifundia (similar to plantations). Because the agrarian holdings of the elite were exceedingly large to be worked by a single tenant family and traditional workers were leaving the land in great numbers, the supply of labor dwindled. In the absence of domestic supply of labor, the elites turned to captives of war, who had been spared (*servi*) to resuscitate the moribund agrarian economy. This made it necessary for the exploitation of the slaves in the provinces to be much more severe and merciless.

Chattel slavery was an extreme type of compulsory forced labor. It created a hostile atmosphere with opportunities for rebellion and conflagration. This atmosphere was explosive, and its stability, for the most part, depended on intimidation, control, and sustained subjection. These were all ensured by positive law, and in combination they ensured the exploitation of the slaves.

The Force of Positive Law

Intimidation, control, and prolonged subjection were subsumed in several aspects of the law. By intimidation, I mean the law that induced fear to guarantee humility. Slaves were in the power of their masters, which implied complete disability, both personal and proprietary. The master had "the right of life and death." This should be studied against the ultimate aim of slavery, which is to increase the master's satisfaction in several areas for his consumption and economic betterment, with lesser consideration for the slaves. I have already alluded to the peculium of the slave and the way it could be manipulated. One of the effects of this arbitrary situation is to instill fear and force submission for the master to derive maximum benefits.

The usufructuary rule allowed control over the benefits of slaves or his labor in other ways. The usufructuary rule gave masters a wide latitude over the rewards of labor for service to a third party.[17] The basic picture of acquisition through slaves in classical law is set out by Gaius. He argues that ownership and possession are acquired through those who have been possessed by power, and that whatever slaves acquire through usufruct is acquired by the benefactors.[18]

The Law of Injury (*Inuria*)

When an injury was done to a slave, the right of action would accrue to the master, not to the slave. Slaves were deprived of the right to sue. The *Twelve Tables* of the mid-fifth century B.C. contained provisions on physical injury. The three principal wrongs that could be done to a slave were murder or physical injury, theft, and physical assault. In 287 B.C. Lex Aquilla attempted to regulate damage. Injuries which qualified for legal consideration were those done in violation of some rights, which accrued to the master of a slave when a slave was injured (since the slave was a *res*).[19] Because *actio iniuriarum* could only be brought by the owner, all rewards went to the owner, but the action might be brought *suo nominee*, on the master's account, or *servi nominee*, on the slave's account.

Contracts

Lee points out that the edicts of Roman law do not supply a definition of contract. *Contractus* and *contrahere*, akin to contract in English, are used in various senses. Labeo interprets *contractus* to mean reciprocal obligation; but when obligations become the operative word in contracts, it would seem that the Romans are referring to obligations arising from convention or agreement. The contracts known to Roman law fell in the categories of real, verbal, literal, and consensual. They were either unilateral or bilateral, or formal or informal (informal meaning they might depend on the varying interests of parties); the contract of sale was regarded as informal. *Stipulatio*, which is what was done for establishing a peculium, was in the form of a question and answer. Two issues are recognizable: the promise to give and why. The why issue is irrelevant in formal contracts, but in the informal contracts, the why issue is relevant because informal contracts are called causal contracts.

The contracts have vital elements, of which the contribution of the partners is important. Contribution need not be equal or symmetrical; but when scruples are factored into consideration, each side ought to contribute something. Slaves were deprived of this right, and the Roman law did not attempt to restore it. A contractless labor arrangement was certainly doomed. The Roman law of contracts did not have a general theory. It took special classes of contracts into account, giving selective cognizance to such contracts. Roman slaves could not contract at all because they were destitute of civil capacity to do so. On the contrary, they incurred natural obligation when they entered a contract; whether or not the contract was expressly in the name of the master, the master acquired all rights under the contract. In classical law, acquisition was obtained even when the master was unaware until Justinian reformed it and restricted it to delivery on account of the peculium.

The advantages of using a slave in commerce were far greater than those of using a free person. This is so because the slaves were used as proxy in contracts, which provided the masters with very limited liabilities. Slaves were therefore beneficial to the master in terms of acquiring rights under contracts. The Roman contract of mandate, in which one person contracts on behalf of another, did not directly give the principal an action against a third party who contracted with the mandatory. Gaius indicates that the general picture of acquisitions through slaves was subject to compliance.[20] The slaves can't sue and may not be sued since the contracts were only mutually binding. This was one big avenue, not only to exploit slave labor but the status of slaves. *Operae servarum*, the right to use the services of a slave, guaranteed this utility. This right was governed by the rules of contract.

As we have seen, contract goes *in tandem* with obligation. In the *Institutes*, obligation is a legal bond. It is a *res incorporalis*, which makes it applicable to the law of things, *jus recrum*. Obligation creates a *jus personam*, which is the right available against a specific person. Though the perception of this might be cloudy, as Lee argues, it seems to me it could be made more applicable to slaves who were defined as *res* anyway.

Contracts also were implied. If a slave was emancipated and became a freedman, he was still attached to his master or patron by *obseqium* (respect), *operae* (services), and *bona* (property). These obligations did not espouse independence, but made manumission a nominal phenomenon. The freedman owed respect to his patron and might not bring an action against him. There was also a reciprocal duty of support when a need arose.

After being freed, the freedman was under oath to render services to his patron. This included a fixed number of work days. This was done

19

under *jus jurandum liberti*, and the tasks were frequently onerous. Slaves could not bind themselves by civil law contract for which oath was the viable alternative. The oath was repeated after manumission to create a civil liability which persisted under Justinian.[21]

According to the law of the *Twelve Tables*, the patron gained property of a *libertus*, if the *libertus* died intestate without leaving *sui heredes*, (family heirs). By a later law, he was entitled to take a share of wealth if the freedman had made a will. Justinian legislation, however, nullified this law by denouncing the claim of a patron when children were in existence to the *libertus*.[22]

Sustaining Subjection

To perpetuate the system of moral neglect, it was not only necessary to have laws that would replenish, but ones that would inject a dose of intimidation. The inducement of fear came in many forms, but it was particularly striking in the way it appeared through the laws of manumission. The way a slave was freed impinged on the relationship with his master— because it was the master who really decided the secondary status of a slave after emancipation—something that indubitably warrants good behavior.

As a legal institution, Roman slavery was comprehensive when one realizes the ambition of the slave to be free within the limits allowed by law to become "Roman citizen." Though some had chances to be free, there were those who did not have the ghost of a chance to change their status because of the whims of their masters. Manumission was only recognized when it was done within the limits of law. When it was not, the status of the slave was imperilled and the benefits to the master colossal.

From Gaius's *Institutes* an insight is given to the legal considerations of the law for freeing slaves. First, at age thirty they were expected to be free; second, the slave must have been owned by a Roman; and, third, he could only be freed by a statutorily recognized medium—namely, *vindicta*, census, or testament. All other methods would make the slave a Latin.[23] *Vindicta* is a juristic dodge of a fictional character, otherwise known as "the claim for freedom"—*vindicatio in libertatem*. A master wishing to free his slave made arrangement with a third party to bring a suit against him in front of a magistrate, claiming that he had wrongfully held his slave in bondage. Long before Justinian, this was a mere formality. The census involved the formal enrollment of the slave with the owner's consent on the census list of Roman citizens; like the *vindicta*, it also operated on a fraudulent scheme (sometimes for the same reason). The testament did not involve any dodge. A slave belonging to a testator could be given freedom directly by a testament. It should, however, be noted that freedom was normally conditional. A slave given freedom on grounds of conditionality, *statuliber*, remained in bondage until the condition was fulfilled.

When conditionality is imposed, usually of a pecuniary variety, the slave was at the mercy of the testator or the heirs of the testator.

Buccaneering masters had the option of not selecting any of the above to hold the slave in perpetual bondage. They were in bondage because even when they were freed without the recognized process, their Latinity accrued tremendous profits to their (former) masters. Masters were inheritors of the property of Latins. Although the praetor saw to it that slaves received protection from their masters, the death of a Latin facilitated the transfer of property, including the peculium to the master. The children of the freed Latin were excluded from succession. This process of transfer was modified by a senate decree to apportion estates.

The general rule of *jus gentium* was that children followed the status which their mother had at the time of birth (contrary to the rule that when the parents had *an offspring* and were lawfully married, the issue followed the status of the father at the time of conception). [24] Though there were some exceptions from the general rule, they were repealed by Hadrian and Vespasian. This made it possible for the perception of *jus gentium* to prevail irrespective of who was a Latin. Roman slavery essentially reproduced itself to maintain the *status quo* in the period under review.

Concluding Remarks

I have referred to a broad spectrum of events, ranging from the sixth century B.C. to the time of Justinianus. The emphasis on law during this period is significant in all senses. No doubt law started off as customary. Predicated on *jus gentium*, law legitimized the ordered hierarchy of society. It defined status and obligations. In short, it became the trajectory that facilitated the exploitation of labor, where exploitation is indicative of the advancement of a particular class at the expense of the other. Lack of scruples attended this organization, not only because little consideration was given to normative questions, but because the age itself could be defined in terms of greed and the factors or instruments needed to sustain it.

The control of labor was absolute and coercive because this is the nature of slavery. Slaves were *res*, things of economic value with no control over their own labor in any sense. The laws aided exploitation on the following fronts. First, the nonstatus or "bi-status" worked to exploit the slaves; contracts were formal, informal, or implied, and there were judicial obstacles, intimidation, and a system of replenishment.

In the Roman law of slavery we see an interesting manifestation of justified injustice. This is so because there is almost always a tendency to justify positive law on a moral ground. The Romans made an appeal to *jus gentium*, which is thought to be what all nations should obey because of its natural qualities.

In the next chapter, I will deal with the serfs. I will focus on how, in actual fact, they were confronted with the circumstance of feudalism and how, in a similar way but with changing conditions, the law became an impediment to the personal control of their rewards from labor. In other words, I will show how the law really ensured injustice in economic relations.

Chapter 2

The Serfs

Now I plan to look at feudalism with some of its nuances in Western Europe. Feudalism in Western Europe is a modified rather than a unique system. This is so because the feudalism I am referring to evolved over time and became a blend of different cultures, predominantly that of the Romans and the Barbarians who subjugated the western portion of the Roman Empire. Thus far, we can anticipate that relics and tradition were bound to be a part of this kind of arrangement. It came into existence not because there was an attempt to morally reform ancient slavery, but because a change in political and economic circumstances within the Roman empire necessitated the adjustment. It is against this background that feudal justice or *justitia* should be understood. Therefore, when mention is made of feudal law, aspects of Roman law will be subsumed.

The Advent of Feudalism and the Insignificance of an Ancient Slave Owning System

Beginning with the third century, it was apparent that the Roman authority over Europe was moribund. As the volume of trade decreased within the empire, money circulation was reduced, the population dwindled, and, because many fled to the country, towns fell into a state of neglect. When the Barbarians overran the western portion of Rome in A.D. 476, some historians suggest a long foundering process came to head. The cumulative effect of economic reverses made Rome poorer and brought attention to the need for structural adjustment at the economic level.

One of the significant causes for economic malaise was an unfavorable balance of trade that Italy suffered in her commerce with the provinces. To check the withdrawal of precious metals from the country, the government did not encourage manufacture for export, but resorted to an expedient of debasing coinage (devaluation). Nero started the debasing, but his successors continued until the proportion of baser metal in Roman coins increased to 98.5 percent. The ultimate disappearance of money meant a number of things. For example, government intervention, which came in the form of decrees binding peasants to the soil and compelling every townsman to follow the occupation of his father, became necessary to ensure the continuation of production.

The old slave-owning system was caught in disarray. Slave revolts and epidemics, in addition to economic adversity, liquidated the shareholders and weakened the institution of slavery as the fundamental source of exploitation. What did take place was the replacement of slave holders with feudal landlords and a change in the complexion of exploitation to patch up an order that had disintegrated.

The adjustment was a necessary one. Food was scarce and bondage to the land inevitable if people were to survive. The inadequacy of slave labor, which contributed to the situation, made it difficult for the owners of large estates or latifundias to supply food to the city markets. Instead, the owners rented the land out to small tenants who did not have the enabling factors to increase productivity. The reliance on subsistence agriculture further exacerbated the grip of inflation; even the great estates restricted production to self-consumption.

The economy of the ancient world lost the stimulus of expansion. The Romans made no significant inventions of machinery to accelerate production. Wealth, which was concentrated in a few aristocratic hands, was quickly squandered and invested in large, landed estates, rather than in commerce and industry.

In panic and confusion, the government's fiscal policies hastened the advent of a changed order. Diolectian (A.D. 284-305), for example, imposed taxes on land and encouraged the breakup of lands into units of varying sizes, with exactions on municipalities to come up with specific amounts. The tax system was regressive because peasants, not the great land owners, had to pay the tax. Many peasants suffered under the inexorable weight of taxation and had no alternative but to abandon their land.

From some of the laws made by Constantine, we learn that no matter who owned the land the worker remained hereditary tenant, legally free but unable to leave the land (*coloni*). Slaves were no longer to be sold off the land to which they were bound, and as their value as saleable property disappeared, they were afforded the partial value of *coloni*. All farm workers were levelled to the same condition of partial servitude. Like a fugitive slave, the colonus was punished with the same severity for abandoning land. By the fourth and fifth centuries workers on land had been degraded, the merchant and artisan classes had fallen into comparative insignificance, and the middle and upper classes of the municipalities were being persecuted. The class that was well ensconced was the "nonproductive" senatorial aristocracy.

Progressive deterioration culminated in very weak central governments between the eighth and ninth centuries. As land became the main source of wealth, governments deprived of financial support were forced to pay for services with grants of land or to delegate duties and privileges to those land holders who could exert effective authority over the people on their land. Weakened by civil wars and rebellions, the later rulers were unable to protect their people from raids by the northmen (often times referred to as Barbarians), nor could these rulers prevent or control the violence of the nobles.[25]

The nobles escaped punishment for a few reasons. In the absence of a central militia, they became the fighting aristocracy, and not only the government but also peasants came to rely on their protection. The great landlords, having gained control over a body of serfs, entrenched themselves on their estates, openly defied government, and ruled as feudal magnates. What really changed from the old order were the economic conditions, but not the economic relations embodied in lordship and vassalage.

Two essential developments are particularly noteworthy: the *colonate* and *patronate* systems. The great estates based on slave labor ceased to bring in income, and small holdings became profitable. These small holdings were leased out to hereditary free tenants or debtors, who paid the landowner a certain share of crop every year because of the virtual collapse of the monetary system. The *coloni* were not necessarily former slaves because the *colonate* absorbed even those who had hitherto been free, but who, for nonpayment, lost their independence and freedom.

To protect themselves from judges (or the law) and the violence of officials, the peasants often sought the help of a powerful seigneur or master. Not only did individual peasants engage in this issue, but whole communities also adopted the same practice. As a condition of his patronage, the patron demanded the transmission of the ownership of land from the peasant to him, with the assurance that the peasant would use the plot for life. The *patronate* gave power to the landed magnates, who used the arrangement for economic and political power, because land and power were virtually synonymous. Inherent in feudalism was a system of sub-infeudation, whereby the great nobles who had fiefs directly from the king were able to split the greater parts of their lands into smaller fiefs and grant them to vassals who thus became sub-vassals of the king. The sub-vassals themselves could have "sub-sub-vassals." This process came into existence as a result of a vast number of bargains and agreements between private individuals, or between individuals and the monarch, in which both parties made the best terms they could according to their needs and ambitions.

Before venturing into sources of feudal law or the origins of this arrangement, I will first discuss the general framework within which feudalism should be understood. There are basically three essential factors: decentralization, land ownership, and role specialization. These form the basis for the making and interpretation of feudal law. They meant obedience, contract, and punishment for the dereliction of duty.

Land was transferred by hereditary right from a social superior to a vassal or serf in return for personal services, with few exceptions of private ownership. Decentralization here refers to the detachment of the citizenry from the government and the ordinary rights and duties of government. The government was more or less represented in the nobles who performed a variety of functions the government should have been performing, such as law enforcement and the provision of a centralized militia.

Sources of Feudal Law

To understand the feudal legal setup, it is highly relevant to understand the merger of Roman and Germanic culture in Europe. When I say Germanic, I allude to the input of those who were so-called "Barbarians." By doing so, we will be tracing an admixture of sources which has baffled many scholars and researchers as to the origin of the feudal practice and what sources should be accorded primacy.

Libri Feudorum

During the eleventh century, ordinances had been promulgated by the rulers of the Italian kingdom (who were in fact German kings). These ordinances gave rise to a collection of technical literature, which apart from providing commentaries on the law, describes "the good customs of the courts." The most important chapters of this literature were compiled in what became known as *Libri Feudorum*.[26]

From the *Libri Feudorum*, we learn that the oath of fealty appears to suffice as the basis of allegiance and that homage of mouth and hands is not mentioned.[27] The significance here is that obligations were contracted without any formal act.

The Scottish historian Sir Thomas Craig, who published the *Jus Feudale* in 1603, saw in the *Libri Feudorum* a systematic exposition of the principles of tenure, forfeiture, and inheritance under a single rule, or to the point where a single code of law could be drawn up and prove of some use.

The *Libri Feudorum* portrays also, as Sir Henry Spelman points out, that feudal law upheld a hierarchial system imposed from above as a matter of policy.[28] Hence, for the most part, land was granted to the great nobles not for their personal enjoyment, but for the provision of soldiers as defenders of the realm.

Spelman states in the *Archaelogus* that when felony (*felo, felonia*) was used in the *Libri Feudorum*, it was used in a feudal sense to convey a dereliction of duty, for which the vassal suffers reprisal by forfeiting his fee.

The *Libri Feudorum* is the only written systemization of feudal law, developed from unwritten custom. Though the laws contained within it were hardly enforceable anywhere, they had doctrinal authority in most places where feudalism was found to be in existence. The *feudum*, like slavery, was held to be akin to *jus gentium.*[29] It was a universal institution considered to be formed by nature and affirmed by decrees which possessed the stature of universal law. According to J.G.A. Pocock, "they were in effect if not formally, part of the *Corpus Juris Civilis,* and as such were glossed by the Bulgarus in the thirteen century and were the subject of *Summae* by Hugolinus and Odofredus, and *Commentarii* by Baldus, Jason and others."[30]

Gerardus Niger, supposed author of the first of the *Libri Feudorum,* describes feudal law as "antiquissium." He was himself a Lombard who was less inclined to be parochial. He attributed the *Libri Feudorum* to something that evolved through several distinct stages from tenure at will to life tenure. He warns that it will be a mistake to seek feudalism's origins from the Lombards or the Goths, whose laws contain no comprehensive allusion to *feuda*; nor could it be described as "antiquissium" unless it could be convincingly linked with the institutions of the Roman people.

The Barbarian Laws and Customs

Unlike the Roman law, little publicity was given to the "Barbarian Laws" (which were really codes of laws and customs of the Germans) until after the subjugation of the Western Empire in A.D. 476. Barbarian incursions into the empire had been sporadic but noticeable, even before the fourth century. Though such incursions were successfully dispelled before the fourth century, it became increasingly difficult thereafter for various reasons, some of which have already been highlighted. Mass invasion began in 376 when the Visigoths crossed the Danube River. This precedent was followed by other tribes of the northern frontier. The successive waves across the shattered frontier culminated in the 476 debacle.

The codes of Barbarian laws began to appear from the fifth century. Their contents are reflective of German codes of law and customs going back to the second and third centuries. There is very deep economic differentiation in these laws at the village level; for example, the rich owning large allotments of land (most of which came from the king) were able to recruit slaves for labor, while they were charged with the responsibility of providing military services.

All lands of the vanquished were declared king's property, a portion of which went to military leaders.[31] They built a class society defined with some confusion into nobles, freemen, freedmen and slaves. The family was a social unit, but custom allowed large kinship groups. Members of a clan felt mutual responsibility for the welfare of their fellows and supported them in lawsuits or battle. This clannish loyalty was useful for protection of individuals at a time when government was incompetent. Distinct from these family or kinship groups was the *comitatus*, a band of warriors who attached themselves voluntarily to chiefs renowned for courage and skill in war.

The smallest political unit was the village community, which enjoyed a considerable degree of self-government in the unsophisticated way; the government was in the hands of a council of chiefs. The social and political ideas of early Germans were closely affiliated with family relationships or personal loyalties to the chief or king. The villages consisted of tribes or *Pagi,* which were extended into kindreds and economic units for production.

The Barbarian laws dealt with injuries and obligations. But unlike later Roman law, they were not the product of legislation on the part of the government or precedents established by judges. They were made up of immemorial customs of the tribes that were handed down from generation to generation. They were not written until after the invasion (something which probably prompted Justinianus to do the same on the East).[32]

In the *Germania*, produced in A.D. 98, Tacitus cites the leader of the Visigoths as a judge, with the obvious implication that he performed some judicial functions.[33] Some judicial matters were in the hands of leading men of each people. Though they did not have compelling rights to summon miscreants, they could use the influence they possessed to settle the matter.

The Barbarian form of slavery, according to Tacitus, was subtly different from that of the Romans and had some preconditions for feudalism. Slaves had their own homes separate from their masters, and were obliged to pay to their masters at intervals quantities of grain, cloth, or head of cattle. The masters, we are informed, also had judicial powers, one of which empowered them to put slaves to death with impunity.

What I have attempted to do so far is to identify a major source from which the practice of feudalism was likely to have ensued. In the course of the tenth century, the Barbarian laws gradually fell into a state of oblivion. It should be noted that Roman law never totally fell into desuetude, even after the Barbarian conquest. Notice also that some of the Barbarians who had been sojourners in the West were also accustomed to Roman practices and laws, so that when the Barbarian codification was jump-started after the conquest, Roman law was not disregarded altogether. The task of feudalism was as much to compromise between these two cultures as it was to absorb the interjections of the church. Indeed, Roman law was a significant component of the *Libri Feudorum*.

The Carolingian Capitularies

During the eighth century, there was an alliance of Frankish kings with the Roman Pope to restore the fortunes of the old Roman Empire in the West. By so doing, three elements—the Gemanic, Roman, and Christian traditions—were united to form the epitome of medieval civilization. These are in fact the crucial elements defining feudalism in Western Europe. Although the Carolingian Empire lasted less than a century, it had an indelible impact on the way feudalism came to be known in Western Europe, for medieval institutions felt the all pervasive impact of the church, not only in matters of faith, but also in terms of pecuniary and physical exactions levied on peasants. England fell under the yoke of this trinity in 1066 when the Normans conquered it.[34] There seems to be some correlation between Lombard law and *Libri Feudorum*, for according to the Scottish historian, Craig, Charlemagne must have discovered it in operation when he conquered the Lombard Kingdom, and it must have been from this source that it spread to the rest of the Frankish Empire. The Carolingian capitularies were decrees from the kings covering varied aspects of public and private life, religion and morality, church and state. They detail "among others" institutions for the management of the royal estates. They were supposed to be a recipe for improving feudal productivity and drawing income from land. The capitularies dealing with the management of royal estates were copied on the great villas or estates of the nobles and the church. Large estates were created during this period as small landowners lost land and freedom because of compulsory military service.

Carolingian ordinances did not continue the Roman system of direct taxation. Among Frankish principal sources of income was the exploitation of the domains of the royal treasury. Charlemagne in the spring of 802 redefined the oath of fealty to include nothing against the interest of the king—even in revenue collection. It was in actual fact the Carolingian rearrangement and capitularies that defined feudalism within the political concepts in which we have come to understand it today. Stephenson clarifies:

> By feudalism . . . we properly refer to the peculiar associations of vassalage with fief-holding that was developed in the Carolingian Empire and hence spread to other parts of Europe.[35]

Vassalage first appears as a prominent institution in the Carolingian official enactments. It was the Carolingian policies that established legal precedents which came to be observed for many centuries.

29

Applications of Feudal Law

The binding force of feudal institutions was an oath, something of an equivalent to modern contract in the workplace. The oath was what bounded the serf to the lord and the lord to the vassal. The serf, on the one hand, swears to be faithful and diligent to the lord, and the lord, on the other hand, reciprocated by guaranteeing the protection of the serf. F.L. Ganshof dates the practice to the second half of the eighth century and part of the ninth century. Those entering into the band of vassalage took an oath of fealty. The term *fidelitas* was used to describe what was sworn, although *fides* was also apparent for the same reason. We have already seen how the old order disintegrated, how the supply of labor dwindled, and what made ancient slavery within the Western Empire an obsolete phenomenon. The arrangement which supplanted slavery made the serf the possessor of his means of production. In other words, he conducted his own economy, but in doing so he was obligated to give part of his time or part of the product of labor or wages to the lord. This portion that was allotted in extraneous ways to his lord made it impossible for him to fend totally for his subsistence. Deprivation here is not only of labor time spent, but even the rewards for labor were sources of exactions. The incubus was of three dimensions: the lord, the church, and the state all looking for revenues from the serf. This was the greatest burden on the serf.

Commendation

Commendation was an act acknowledged by law to cover different forms of personal subordination.[36] It was often times the product of poverty, whereby a poor man or debtor surrendered himself to a lord to perform services of a very humble character. According to long established custom, a lesser freeman could become the client of any wealthy Roman who agreed to be his patron. The client was essentially an economic dependant, and it was not always the case that he had to perform military services. Since the very practice was used to avoid military services, commendation was used to ensure, in the most effective manner possible, the fulfilment of duties by the vassals. *Commendatio* appeared in the laws of the visigothic king, Euric, in fifth century Gaul. Since it was legally a contract of some sort, abrogation of it was punishable by a fine called *solidi*. The agreement contained a *dispositio* (a dispositive clause in which its author expresses his will) and a *narratio* (which is the narrative portion of the act, intended to explain and justify the dispositive clause). Whosoever commended himself had an obligation to serve and respect his master, with the understanding that faithfulness would ensure the status of a freeman. Many great landowners took advantage of their power and lack of governmental control to force poorer neighbours into this dependent situation.

Vassalage

By the eighth century, vassalage, as a Roman or a German custom, had long been recognized as established law. Charles Martel, Pepin, and Charlemagne adopted pragmatic approaches in defending their extensive empire, and it was from their enactments that vassalage made the earliest appearance as a prominent institution. The origin of vassalage is shrouded in controversy, but its operative practice suggests employment on government missions for which the rewards were benefices, which were estates carved out of the royal domain or confiscations from the church. The status of the vassal was higher than the peasant, since he was normally considered a fighter of excellence (whether in the employment of the king or not).

The significance of vassalage to feudalism is the reward system that came to be attached to it. The connection really clarified our understanding of what we mean by feudal tenure today. The old Frankish army was made of ordinary freeman who provided their own weapons and served without pay. The Carolingians, in the process of expanding their fighting capacity and encouraging it to be more effective, associated vassalage with benefice-holding as a matter of reciprocation for labor services. This reciprocation was known as military benefice or fief because of the inability to pay cash remuneration for military labor.[37]

It seems to me, therefore, that the benefice system which operated under the old Frankish kingdom should be studied with some precaution when mapping our current analysis of feudal tenure and the benefice system as they operated after the Carolingians. At times "benevolence" attended the practice in the Frankish era, for the benefice was normally held with the principle of *ius in re aliena*, the right over a thing belonging to another. This was usually an usufructuary mechanism of deriving benefits for the church and was not entirely benign. The Carolingian vassal acquired immunities with his fief, including the administration of justice and collection of fines and taxes, so that absolute power, and later absolute corruption, hastened the financial misery of the peasant's exploitation. Notice that it was also possible for someone to be a vassal without owning a fief. The Carolingian capitularies refer to nonbeneficient vassals who lived in their lord's households. Exceptional as this was, it was also possible for a man to become a vassal without receiving a fief. But a fief could legally exist only when held by a vassal. The legality of the practice of vassalage owes its recognition to the force of law by homage and the oath of fealty.

Feudal and Seignorial Justice/*Justicia*

Seignorial justice was justice administered over nonvassals, rather than that perceived in terms of arrangement between vassals and lords and the judicial rights afforded the lord as an owner of a fief. Through the acquisition of a fief, the lord obtained the right to administer justice, not through his personal control over vassals, but through his acquisition of a fief. The fief brought him political authority because it epitomized a particular immunity. Seignorial government operated on the basis of devolution. Feudal justice was differentiated for the benefit of the military class. The vassal was exempted from a system of judicial extortion which descended vigorously on the defenseless peasantry. The law which regulated vassal behavior was that made by a truly feudal court, the composite of which were vassals or the peers of vassals. Feudal trials expressed two main characteristics: trial by combat and condemnation for felony. Felony is a pronouncement based on dereliction to perform military services, to attend to a lord's court, or, in short, a breach of oath which had punitive repercussions like fines or the forfeiture of land. Oath is therefore the fulcrum on which feudal jurisdiction rests.

It would seem that the further disintegration of the state during the chaotic years of the ninth and early tenth centuries made it possible for the lords to have considerable judicial powers over their vassals because the early and greater part of the Carolingian period did not provide for the lord to be a judge of his vassal.

In France the territorial prince and counts set out to create for themselves *curias* (courts) based on the royal model or the Carolingian county model during this period. Similarly, in England after the Norman Conquest, great and lesser lords established courts with jurisdiction over matters of vassalage and fiefs, although their stature was subsequently challenged by policies of the crown from the second half of the twelfth century. The degeneration of the legal system, however, gave the lords considerable power over their serfs, who became thoroughly vulnerable in legal matters. The Norman period in England and France during the eleventh century made provisions for appeal. This form of appeal, according to Bloch, known as "suing the judge," existed as early as the epoch of Barbarian kingdoms.[38] It was a dangerous adventure, for the proof of vindication depended on trial by combat.

The right to adjudication was dispersed and uncontrollable. Feudalism was, by nature, hostile to a central government. And since all local government were in the hands of nobles, private jurisdictions became instrumental in the utilization of labor. Every noble had full jurisdiction within his own fief and exercised the power of government. Nobles levied taxes through tolls on roads and bridges and could always raise an army of vassals to accomplish numberless objectives—hence the prosecution of private wars which attended the feudal regime. Whoever found himself the master of a small group of humble dependents and derived rents and services from a small group of rural tenements possessed at least the right of "low justice" ("high justice" being confined to the prosecution of purely criminal matters). Low justice was jurisdiction over a territory over which one had control. Rights of high justice incorporated that of low justice, but not conversely. Low justice included the trial of all disputes between the lord himself and his tenants, particularly as it related to the obligation of the tenants. Its real source was predicated on the conception of "the powers proper to the chief," which engendered a right to exactions from an inferior. Knowledge of this practice in twelfth century France came through as *justice fonciere*. Whoever exercised the right of low justice practically adjudicated all civil actions, which could be classified within the limits of his control and therefore not *ultra vires*.

The right to judge and sentence the peasants together with the collection of duties and fines weighed heavily on the peasants. The lack of mechanisms to check the lord's excesses made it easy for the lord to overstep the lawful limits of exactions. This is one aspect of feudal structure that never changed all over Western Europe. As the lords learned to perpetrate their illegitimate acts, they began to issue edicts and ordinances when old customs challenged their interests. These capitularies were not normally issued on a personal basis, but by a congress of vassals on an *ad hoc* basis. The codes of feudal laws contain numerous lists of all lands of fines. Apart from everything else, the feudal courts were agents of profit that gained blessings from kings for the most part. Kings gave judges power to exact fines in nearly all cases examined in court. Grotesque situations and travesties arose; for example, whole communities were fined for the "misconduct" of a single individual. It is therefore not surprising that feudal justice, *justitia*, was to a large extent the mirror of the lord's power as a whole.[36] The judicial power of the lords was not new. At its worst, it must have been an atavism—a throwback to the Roman period when masters, with their own courts and prisons, became self-made judges over slaves.

The failed judicial system had ripple effects. The judicial set up clearly did not protect the peasant from exaction or acts of violence. This led peasants to pursue insurance policy to shield themselves against the very thing that was supposed to protect them—law. The insurance policy itself, which was known as the *patronate*, involved a great measure of deprivation of land. To protect themselves from the wrath of judges and the violence of officials, the peasants often sought the help of a powerful seigneur, who was usually a master of whole counties. As a precondition for patronage, the patron demanded a peasants's land, which on a de facto basis the peasant would be allowed to farm for life. The patron became the ultimate authority over his dependents. He established his own courts, built jails, and transformed his estate into a small independent state. A.I. Gucovsky records that "(the patron) drove the emperor's tax collectors away and squeezed a lot out of the population."[40] This system enhanced the opportunities of patrons to get rich at the expense of their dependents, who were armed for the economic benefits of the patrons. It was an arrangement of great impediment to the centralization of states that, with the support of law, facilitated exploitation of labor.

Concluding Remarks

Feudalism should be seen as a patchwork of a bygone, demoded order, a hierarchial complex of bonds between men and the soil which derived its sanctity from a remote mix of Roman and Barbarian culture. The disintegration of the state produced an alternative in the persons of nobles, who carved out their own petty political enclaves and used the labor of peasants with little or no state interventions. The serf became different from the slave in that the serf possessed his means of production and conducted his own economy. Yet he was obliged to give part of his time or product to his lord, the church, and the state.

The feudal order, like the one that preceded it, was an order of laws. The laws were more often than not tangential to the interests of the serfs but amiable to the interests of the nobles. The real function of laws, as the applications show, was to maintain an order in which kings depended on the nobles, or rather, an order that could not control the nobles. Justice was a lucrative device for creating wealth and sustaining the status quo. Fusion of powers is embodied in the nobles: they made laws, interpreted them, and enforced them. The atmosphere was intimidating and the quest for wealth insatiable. The returns for labor were obviously not commensurate to the work performed, and the hours for work were arbitrary and functionally related to the pressures on the peasant to produce in order to offset debts. Lesser time was allocated by the peasant to the production for his subsistence, and this is one major proof that the arrangement was exploitative.

Labor contracts were based on the oath of fidelity or fealty, which were centerpieces of judicial action. Fealty originated as a customary practice. It subsumed a lot and gave the lords exceeding power to extort from their peasants under the cardinal principles of homage and submission. It said nothing about the number of hours to be worked but something about rewards for and protection of the serf. In addition to other tasks, peasants were allocated a week of work per month to the lord's demesne, for, like the slave, the serfs possessed economic value. Yet the realization of such value was impeded by the imposition of oppressive laws. Remonstrance against the immorality of law was periodic, but it was not until the 1789

34

conflagration in France that the legitimacy of the ancient regime was challenged on an unprecedented scale.[41] This uprising was to shape the political and social history of Europe in the subsequent years, aided by the Industrial Revolution, which had already taken place prior to the outburst of the revolution.

Chapter 3

The American Slaves

Sources of American Slave Law: A Case Study of Modern Slavery and Law

The institution of American slavery that preceded the Civil War was a peculiar one—more of a Southern institution. It came into existence with mixed conceptions and struggled for legitimacy in a country where the legal basis for its practice was thoroughly controversial. Supporters of slavery found justification for it in the ancient document of Roman law. By the time modern slavery gained momentum in America, ancient slavery and serfdom in Western Europe had provided very good repositories of knowledge, but there were serious constitutional problems emanating from colonial constitutional prescriptions and the issue of custom in America.

In 1547 a statute of enslavement was introduced in England under Edward VI as a punishment for idleness and vagabondry, but it was repealed two years later. Before the 1772 proclamation of Chief Justice James Mansfield, there was no clear indication that English law recognized slavery. Between 1578, when Queen Elizabeth issued a patent to Sir Humphrey Gilbert granting him the exclusive right to "inhabit and possess at choice all remote and heathen lands not in the actual possession of any Christian prince," and 1606, when concessionaires of Sir Walter Raleigh obtained a charter from James I, the understanding was that colonies should enact no laws that contravened the common law, the colonial constitution, and the fundamental laws of Britain. In fact, this was the principle that was supposed to regulate subsequent companies.[42]

Chief Justice Mansfield in the 1772 Somerset case established the repugnance with which English law held slavery. He held that there was not and never had been any legal slavery in England. Granville Sharpe and many others on his side understood the ruling to be applicable to all British colonies as it was in the mother country. The question, as the Chief Justice summarized it, was whether the owner had a right to detain a slave for sale at a foreign land (Jamaica).[43] The answer established and pronounced a common law of England.

The problem of slavery in America was whether it had any basis, any foundation that could legitimize it and circumvent the English common law tradition. Was slavery a customary matter? The first act of the legislature of the province of Virginia on the subject of slavery was passed in 1670 concerning the Indians. One of its provisions, according to Judge Tucker, prohibited free or freed Indians from purchasing Christian servants. The implication here is a simple one. For someone to be emancipated, he must be enslaved first. This leaves us with the inference that at a particular point in time, the Indians were enslaved. If this is so, could slavery only exist by force of positive legislation? U.B. Phillips is skeptical about the Mansfield decision, and he holds it to be in error. The mistake lies in historical invalidity, because the institution in the American community was first established by custom alone and was merely recognized by statutes when they were enacted.[44]

A Maryland act of 1663 states that:

> All negroes or other slaves within the province, and all negroes and other slaves to be hereafter imported into the province, should serve *durante vita*; and all children bearing any negro or other slave, shall be, slaves as their fathers were for the term of their lives.[45]

This suggests that somehow the practice had been familiar to America even before the Mansfield proclamation. The Chief Justice in his charge to the jury in the Bell v. Dalby case alludes to slavery as an antiquated practice.[46] Since it is recognized as a universal practice in America and consistent with the principles of nature, it is a law of the land.

The issue of slavery in the colonies is one in which the authority of the British government was summarily defied from time to time. The Barbados, for example, saw one of the earliest and definite slave regimes, with enacted laws going back to 1644. These laws concerned control of negroes and white servants who were recaptured; they gained a reputation so poignant that they subsequently were copied in 1712 by the South Carolina assembly and by other colonies.

Slavery as a social institution in America then was accepted in the English colonies without any statutory authorization from the parent country. Slavery law came into being bit by bit by statute, judicial precedent, and sometimes based on what people did. Statutes on slavery, like other legal matters, were not made in England, but in the local legislatures. In the process of making laws, judges were equally obligated and therefore had to make new laws. Since slavery laws had existed in ancient Rome, judges turned for direction and guidance to Roman law; the most well-known contemporary accounts of this were Thomas Cooper's *Institutes of Justinian* and John Taylor's *Elements of the Civil Law* (1755).

The Franco-Roman Nexus

France in the seventeenth through the early eighteenth century well could have conceded to the Mansfield decision there was no slavery law. At this time, France readily received Roman law, and this significantly influenced this country's customary practices. Gaps in France's laws, emanating from inadequate customary information, were informally filled by the use of Roman law. Neither royal ordinances, *contumes*, nor the law for French overseas possession, *Contume de Paris*, contained anything about slavery law. Since it was French practice to look to Roman law in order to develop private law, the French saw the solution to the problem of slavery law in Roman law.

From France came extensive royal legislation, in which principles of Roman law preponderated. These laws eventually were brought together and published as the *Code Noir* (Black Code). These laws were made in distant Paris under significantly different conditions for the French American colonies, and they were made by lawyers who had been trained and familiarized with Roman law. The *Code Noir* makes allusions to obseqium (Art. 58) and approval of the king for emancipations. This practice was extended to Louisiana. The law also refers to the peculium and nonpossession of property.

The principle that a slave became free once he or she entered France had been recognized by French jurists since the sixteenth century, though it was not translated into royal decree, and hundreds won their freedom in French courts on the basis of this. Even the king's proposed laws that asked for conditional slavery to exist within his kingdom were rejected by the *Parlement de Paris* (the highest court of France).

The *Code Noir* generally was meant for negro slaves in the colonies, and the *Code Noir* of 1685 recognized negro slavery in French colonies as "necessary and authorized."[*] With no law of slavery in France, France thus acquired slaves in the American possessions before slavery laws existed. Although in Louisiana slavery took its complexion from the *Code Noir* and from usages under "Spanish despotism and superstition," with time, the significance of origin faded in the face of vicious buccaneering practice.

The origin of Spanish slavery law was not materially different from that of the French. Their common denominator was Roman slavery law, with the Spanish focusing more on the Visigothic code and the Justinian variety (the Visigoths, a Germanic tribe, invaded the Roman Empire even though they had sporadic alliances with some Romans). The Roman variety and exigent situations gave rise to a synthesis for regulation.[48]

Watson accedes to the significance of Roman law on two fronts: first, its role in the development of slavery law, and second, the common judicial culture that attended this development, incorporating ideas of judges using some known traditions. Since judges did not possess sweeping rights to innovations, the law of slavery was predominantly statute law because its development was largely a reaction to Justice Mansfield's proclamation.

Historians like Peter Kolchin believe that for analytical purposes, the history of the institution should be divided into two broad chronological categories: the colonial, lasting until about 1770, and the antebellum, beginning about 1800. This distinction is significant because it helps to explain the issue of legitimacy of this peculiar institution during the two periods.[49]

The Early Beginnings of Slavery in America

In America, slave labor formed the basis of the economy and social order. The participation of Englishmen in the slave trade goes back to 1562 when John Hawkins successfully dragooned a group of Africans to be transported to the American colonies.

The supply of labor was scarce, but the economic challenge of production, which was essentially agrarian, was colossal. From S. Hollander, knowledge could be gained about two conflicting dates which marked the introduction of slavery to America by the Portugese—1442 or 1503.[50] It should be noted that the very customary aspect of the practice and its basis in natural law makes it rather futile to pinpoint the date or year in which American slavery started, except to satisfy curiosity or to make very specific arguments. For the intentions of this work, a broad frame of mind will suffice to explain its exploitative nature, as it was guaranteed by law.

Gilbert, Raleigh, and others who followed as promoters of colonies depended on the exploitation of land as their principal source of profit. The resources of English America which were discovered over a period of time required a large supply of labor for their exploitation—a demand that exceeded the supply afforded by the settlers. The most common method of procuring workers adopted by the companies, proprietors, and independent families was a labor contract that was really a stipulation for indenture. The stipulation was that the contractor should transport and maintain a servant for a given term during which the servant was bound to labor for his master. This system had its roots deep in England's aristocratic past, when statutes had provided that laborers must work for fixed wages and that minors between the ages of twelve and twenty-one might be apprenticed by their parents or guardians and thus be obliged to work for a master until they became adults. The procurement of indentured servants for colonization raised new problems concerning the durability of servitude. If a worker was to remain a servant or tenant forever, it was better for him to stay in England and avoid the uncertainties of a wilderness frontier life. At the same time, the turbulent English political setup could not provide an answer. Not only was there political chaos, but the precarious financial position of the fifteenth and sixteenth century monarchs debilitated the strength of the monarchy as an institution. Protracted religious schisms compelled Henry VIII (1509-47), Edward VI (1547—53), Mary Tudor (1553-58), and Elizabeth (1558-1603) to take action. Because the financial status of the monarchy was delinquent, the task of building colonies was left to the pioneers, who were out of harm's way. The crisis of authority between the pioneers and the crown and the companies' need to govern by expediency reenacted aspects of the feudalism that had been common in England.

Theoretically, all land in England and her dominions during this period belonged to the king. He granted individual estates to his subjects and exacted feudal dues and services from the recipients, who were called his tenants in chief or vassals. Prior to 1290, the tenant in charge had the right to subinfeudate, or to exact from a third party the equivalent owed to the king. The statute of *quia emptores* (1290), however, prohibited further subinfeudation by cutting off the intermediary and directing all obligations to the king. This demoded practice, which had fallen into desuetude, was resurrected and extended to the colonies by the charters issued after 1630.[51]

The early charters created two types of land tenure. The Virginia Company, the Massachusetts Bay Company, and the Council for New England did not receive the right to subinfeudate or establish manors. The grantee thus became the tenant, not of the company but of the king. Charters of Maryland, Maine, the Carolinas, and Pennsylvania conferred upon the proprietors the right to sub-infeudate and to create manors and new forms of land tenure.[52] Consequently, the companies applied to four or five American colonies a principle of feudal land law that had been abandoned in England since 1290.

Since the acquisition of labor was costly, companies, rather than exhausting their meager funds, also depended on wealthy emigrants to sustain the colonies by indentured arrangement. After 1629, for example, well-to-do emigrants brought over their families, property, and personal servants to settle in New Haven and Massachusetts. Investors in England who paid the costs of the migration were not incorporated by a royal charter. In New Hampshire, Maine, Maryland, the Carolinas, New Jersey, and Pennsylvania, proprietors and landlords advanced out of their own resources the funds for settling tenants and servants upon their feudal estates. It is from this background that "white" servitude of an indentured manner became prevalent, as each colony at a very early date devised legal codes to govern the indentured servants. It is inaccurate to argue that indentured servitude was entirely white servitude because the first Africans who arrived in Virginia on Dutch Men-of-War in 1619 were apparently incorporated into the colony's labor force as indentured servants, with the understanding of eventual manumission after a period of service.[53] After 1619, slaves subsequently were imported sporadically, and little thought was given to the exact legal status of slaves. It was not until after the mid- seventeenth century that the House of Burgesses passed a legislation referring explicitly to slaves; this occurred years after the viability of tobacco production had been discovered in Virginia. The economic windfall precipitated the need for legitimacy and brought into sharper focus the obscurity of the institution. Even Georgia, whose organic law prohibited the act of slavery, eventually succumbed to it.

The institution of slavery in America, then, owes its origin neither to American nor European legislation. For this reason, the courts became perplexed and confused in the ensuing years as to its legal origin. W. Goodell points out that Roman civil law or feudal law could not comprehensibly or cohesively justify slavery because of the apparent dearth of information, nor could it really matter because the courts of the South could not recognize feudal law as a source of binding definition.[54] In one of many celebrated cases, Harvey and others v. Decker and Hopkins, the court held that slavery is condemned by the laws of nature and could only exist through municipal regulations which were missing on the statute book.[55]

Unfree labor or slave labor, therefore, sought legitimacy to give sanctions and assurances to racial and industrial adjustments already in operation. As a rule, slave-holding colonies (and later states) adopted early in their career a series of laws which were limited in scope to meet and define issues as they were encountered. Accumulated experience showed American communities that slavery posed a general problem of regulation, for which legislatures passed acts of many clauses to define the status of slaves, provide the machinery of their police, and prescribe legal procedure in cases concerning them as property or as persons. Somehow slaveholders manipulated English common law, which did not recognize slavery to justify the institution. The pioneers of this onslaught were men of money and power, who overturned statutes that have inveighed against the practice. States suddenly became vulnerable, for example, Georgia after 1776. Before I venture further, notice that the acquiescence made the practice of slavery tolerable. In the words of J.D. Wheeler:

> In all governments in which the municipal regulations are not absolutely opposed to slavery, persons already reduced to that state may be held in it. [Assuming it a first principle],... slavery has been permitted and tolerated in all colonies established in America by European powers, most clearly as it relates to the blacks and Africans, and also in relation to Indians, in the first periods of conquest and colonization.[56]

In Chapter 1, I mentioned the efficacy of law in regulating social relations of labor. Ancient as this order was, it was not otherwise different from modern slavery. The success of modern slavery, like its ancient counterpart, depended on the efficacy and dexterity of laws to keep a volatile situation in control, a situation which was formulated with the express purpose of maximizing the use of labor under the most egregious conditions. Even though slave holders faced the dilemma of legitimacy, they generally found safe haven in the courts; some judicial decisions, however, disheartened them. The courts were the embodiment of atavisms and saw a legitimacy for order and government in hierarchial societies, irrespective of normative considerations. The exploitation of labor first and foremost was dependent on the definition of status. Who could be classified as a slave?

Applications of Positive Law

Slave labor was used in pitiful circumstances that repudiated natural law. This was facilitated by the idea of chattelhood, which deprived slaves of legal personality but enabled masters to enrich themselves. The process of enrichment was well ensconced and encapsulated by law. First, the law defined the status of slaves.

The Status of Slaves

Although the legal wranglings over the legitimacy of the institution of slavery never subsided, slaves generally were deemed as chattel with varying appendages from "state to state." In Louisiana, there was one noticeable exception; slaves though movable by their nature, were considered immovable by the operation of law.[57] They could be mortgaged, seized, and sold as real estate. By the time slavery took hold in America, slave power had increased and there was a public dimension to the law of slavery. The slave belonged to every citizen; as a result a suspicious fugitive could be interrogated by any citizen and recaptured. Citizen patrols were even organized to preempt or combat escape. The Louisiana statute of June 7, 1806, made slaves real estate to be seized and sold as such. One effect of this inhibited the sale of slaves off the plantations of their masters. The laws of South Carolina, Kentucky, Virginia, and Maryland, to cite some examples, attested to the status of chattelhood. Where there was the absence of written codes like the South Carolina and Louisiana ones, the chattel principle was affirmed and maintained by the courts and included in legislative acts. Goodell brings out the intrusion of Roman civil law into the American order of slavery as existing at an early period, before its modification under professedly Christian emperors. When statutes failed to establish the requisite legal relation, recourse generally was made to Roman civil law.[58]

The declaration of status was the prime precondition for the legal exploitation of slaves. Chattelhood deprived the slaves of all rights except that of testimony in courts under extraordinary circumstances. Other rights or intended rights were hardly enforceable given the high-handed advantages of the slaveholder's control and domination over the slaves.

Slaves could not acquire by purchase or descent, were deprived of heirs, and consequently could not make wills; apart from their peculium, whatever was acquired belonged to the master and slaves had negligible juridical personality. As chattel, slaves could be sold, transferred, or pawned as goods or personal estate. Although Roman slavery did not deprive the slave of education, American slavery placed particular emphasis on the nonprovision of education for slaves (this impacted labor skills in subsequent years after the Emancipation Proclamation).

The legal basis of chattelhood was upheld by the courts for the most part. In the State v. Wagoner, Chief Justice Kinsey of the Supreme Court of New Jersey in 1797 held:

> They [Indians] have so long been recognized as slaves in our law, that it would be as great a violation of the rights of property to establish a contrary doctrine at the present day, as it would in the case of Africans, and as useless to investigate the manner in which they originally lost their freedom" (The State v. Wagoner, 1 Halstead's Reports, 374-378).[59]

Some courts, particularly those of Louisiana, Mississippi, and Kentucky, made an appeal to common law when municipal law was silent. The declared status intimidated the slaves to produce and made for heinous reprisals if they rebelled. The severity of these reprisals could hardly be challenged in the courts of law, given the status of the slaves.

Aggression used in Roman slavery was copied by American slaveholders, and recourse generally was made to the common civil code as containing the true principles of the "peculiar institution." Some legislators authorized the most cruel of outrages, which culminated in the murder of slaves. In South Carolina before 1740, it was not uncommon for owners of slaves to deprive them of limbs or commit other atrocities until whipping was authorized in 1740 to supersede most of the cruel acts. Whipping was neither an entirely good alternative. The Louisiana Civil Code Act 173 suggests that mutilation of slaves was a common practice in the name of chastisement. Slaves were forbidden to resist "lawful commands" of their masters. As usual, the decisions of the courts were consistent with the spirit of the laws. In several cases, including State v. Maner, S.P. Hilton v. Caston, White v. Chambers, and State v. Cheatwood, it was stated that assault and battery could not be committed on the person of a slave, nor was the peace of the state offended for whipping a slave.[60] Slaves were not legally citizens and could not depend upon the law for protection. Even when slaves were hired, their status did not change.

In the State v. Mann, a North Carolina case of December 7, 1829, the defendant, Mann, was indicted for his assault and battery upon Lydia, the servant of one Elizabeth Jones.[61] The defendant, it appeared, had hired the slave for a year, and during that time he chastised her for attempting to escape. The verdict in the lower court favored the State, but Mann appealed, and won. The question before the North Carolina Appellate Court was whether a cruel and unreasonable battery upon a slave by the hirer is indictable. The instruction of the judge to the jury indicated the victim was property, and that the laws of North Carolina uniformly treat the master of a slave as entitled to the same extent of authority as the prime owner. The object in the case was deemed to be the service of the slave, and the hirer became a possessor of both rights and duties in the capacity of the owner. The case reestablished the principle that the power of the master must be absolute to render the submission of the slave perfect. A disunity abrogated the rights of the master and absolved the slave from his subjection. What was really reiterated was inherence in the relationship of master and slave, conferred by the laws of men, if not by the law of God.

The hardship to which slaves were subjected was not always unrestrained by law. For example, laws were made in Mississippi, Alabama, and Missouri to check the unfettered use of authority over slaves. In short, these laws attempted to inject some humanity into a dehumanizing situation. The efficacy of these laws was however doubtful because of the fundamental contradiction of status (for example, the lack of juridical personality and the human condition).

Hours of Work

In the theoretical background, we established that hours-of-work is an important concept because it illustrates the amount of time that the worker is left with to fend for his or her own subsistence when recompense is inadequate. Aided by the law, American slavery greatly depended on the exploitation of labor. The American slaves could not contract on their own behalf, but they could contract as pecuniary agents for their masters. In Chastain v. Brown and other cases, the court instructed the jury that a slave might be the agent of his master, and if his agency was established, the master was bound therein.[62] This is nothing short of puzzling because slaves had no rights of their own, but could act with some legitimate basis for their masters' profits. This case affirmed that a master's interests or convenience could alter the status of a slave in exceptional circumstances. The most pertinent point here is that this function highlights the lack of scruples in labor relations that enhanced returns to the masters through legal prescription.

Responding to the inadequate resting time for slaves, a 1740 act of South Carolina ruled that it was illegal for slaves to work for more than fifteen hours in a twenty-four hour day. The South Carolina act varied the length of work in accordance with the prevailing season. From March 15 to September 25, the law prohibited the slave to work for more than fifteen hours a day. On the other hand, from September 25 to March 25, slaves were not supposed to exceed a maximum of fourteen hours. Violation of this law was punishable by a fine that ranged from five to twenty-five pounds.

Slaves in penitentiaries were equally compelled to work for arbitrary hours, until laws limited labor to ten hours a day in Maryland, Virginia, and Georgia. Though these laws might seem benign today, we can look with retrospect and imagine the anguish these hours of labor could have caused. These were contractless hours of work for a pittance. This problem of hours and wages was not peculiar to the institution of slavery; it resurfaced during the post-Civil War era and created many upheavals as we shall see later.

From a Georgia act of 1817, we learn that these hours of work had not been commensurate to caloric intake. This act emphasized the importance of providing food and nourishment in proportion to labor. Upon sufficient information about violation of the act, the owners of slaves were to be prosecuted before a grand jury. Well-intentioned though the law might have been, it was fraught with insincerity. Its purpose was negated by the very controversial status of slaves.

A July 1806 Louisiana act provided for breaks with seasonal variations, too. In the summer, one half hour was to be set aside for breakfast. From the May to November, two hours were to be allowed for dinner, and from November 1 to May 1, one and a half hours for dinner. The nature of this Louisiana law suggests it was a vestige of Spanish and French law, but in particular it marked an exception to the general pattern of the American slave code. Yet it was not without its flaws. It was equally inimical to the interests of labor by not specifying the hours of work. It was not only nonascertaining in this area, but was silent over the troubling custom of boiling sugar in the night.

What was reckoned in the laws of most states was the apparent paucity or unavailability of laws dealing with the length of the work day. Where there were limitations, they were of no practical significance because of the deprivation of legal status, but also because of the ability of the slaveholders to act collectively.

No Elopement

Today, one of the major strengths of labor is its mobility. Mobility is significant because it is a factor influencing the price of labor. People will migrate to areas of higher wages given the necessary skills. As labor becomes abundant, price falls and the potential for redundance sets in so that there is a sense of equity in a self-adjusting mechanism, albeit with its imperfections. One thing could be established in contemporary labor markets—proprietary rights over this factor of production, at least in democratic societies. But the American slaves had no proprietary rights over their labor. Elopement was a common offense, and fugitive slaves faced serious consequences when apprehended. Not even those who aided and abetted the "offence" were free from the wrath of the law. We already have seen that the arrangement was exploitative. The laws against fugitives were intended to perpetuate the system. In this instance, though, the laws were not using the idea of replenishment directly. By perpetuation, I mean ensuring its continuation at all costs, to the extent of also averting conspiracy for upheaval.

The general rule on the plantation was that slaves must not be absent from "quarters" in the evening, nor was there to be any unceremonious departure. A written pass was the prerequisite for temporary departure. To enforce the law, patrols were established and directed by law in city and county. A slave's inability to give a good account of himself or herself subjected him or her to severe punishment. In Georgia, there was a time when any person could inflict twenty lashes on the bare back of a slave found without license on the plantation or outside the configuration of the town to which he belonged. This application extended to Mississippi, Virginia, and Kentucky at the discretion of a justice. A 1715 Maryland act stressed the requirement of a pass when traveling beyond the limits of a particular county, so that a slave with permission to travel would not be held by a magistrate as a runaway.

The Fugitive Slave Act of 1850 only created havoc for slaves and emancipated negroes who sought to improve their status. The act was a subtle fiat to reenslave. Thus, in the deep South free blacks sometimes reenslaved themselves to selective masters of their choice in order to avoid capture and incarceration.

The U.S. Congress passed two acts to discourage and penalize elopement, one in 1793 and another in 1850, which was repealed in 1864.[63] Before I proceed further, it should be noted that these acts were consistent with the interests of the slave-owning class. The 1793 law enforced Article IV, Section 2 of the U.S. Constitution in authorizing any federal district judge, circuit court judge, or state magistrate in deciding without a jury trial the status of an alleged fugitive slave. The 1793 act was supposed to be a deterrent. Notwithstanding the intention, a significant number of negro slaves escaped via the underground railway to New England or Canada. As a result, the 1850 act made a much more vigorous attempt. Under the 1850 act, fugitives could not testify on their own behalf and were not permitted trial by jury. In addition, heavy penalties were imposed upon federal marshals who refused to enforce the law or from whom a fugitive escaped, and accomplices were punished. The courts also were supportive of masters recapturing their slaves.[64]

State laws were equally intolerant of escape. In South Carolina and Georgia, any person who found more than seven slaves together on the highway without attendance could give each one twenty lashes. A similar law existed in Delaware and in Florida, contrary to the milder code of Spanish slavery previously established in Florida. In Louisiana and Maryland, slaves normally were lashed for playing around facilitators of escape, including horses, dogs, or weapons. It even was legal to put iron chains and collars upon slaves to prevent their escape.[65] In Maryland and the District of Columbia, running into the woods and killing or destroying property without surrender upon pursuance incurred death by shooting. North Carolina and Tennessee enforced a similar law. South Carolina laws went as far as punishing enticement by death, so that a slave could not entice another to escape.

Harboring a slave was a pretty audacious activity. If a free negro concealed or entertained a runaway slave, he was fined ten pounds for the first day and twenty shillings for every succeeding day. Inability to pay the fines and charges involved, as a probable liability, sale into slavery at public outcry (act of 1740).[66] The *Aiken's Alabama Digest* records a fine of up to about seven hundred dollars for concealing a slave.

Concealing is one instance in which the culprit acquired compounded liability as the Scidmore v. Smith case shows.[67] It involved the criminal act remedy, as well as the damages that could be claimed by the master in a civil suit.

We must remember that slaves had economic value to their owners, for which masters even posted "dead or alive" advertisements for missing slaves. The desperation that characterized perpetuity is alarming. Understandably, labor relations formed the backbone of productivity in this agricultural world of the South. Yet with all the atrocities that were endemic, the law was the sustaining force of a system which strove for legitimacy at all costs. This was the system that only war could dismantle.

Replenishment

No system could be sustained unless it could reproduce itself. The extinction of one generation of slavery without replacement would have meant the demise of slavery or serious debilitation of the practice, except there was a means of guaranteeing a smooth supply of labor—i.e., ways of reproducing this means of production. The law became equally important in this area. Law was not a panacea, but it was instrumental in augmenting the source of labor. This was done by fixing the status of the descendants of slaves. This assertion is not new because the Romans tried it; the experiment succeeded in ancient Rome, so why not in the modern era given the identical parameters?

The offspring of slaves born or to be born were declared absolute slaves. According to a South Carolina act of 1740, the status of a mother predetermined the status of her child. A Maryland act of 1715 stipulated that:

> All negroes and other slaves already imported or hereafter to be imported... and all children now born or hereafter to be born of such negroes and slaves, shall be slaves during their natural lives.[68]

Other states with similar stipulations included Georgia (1770), Mississippi (1823), Virginia (1819), and Louisiana. Hereditary status by maternal descent was common to all the slave states. This practice was customary with or without written law. Out of its hereditary transmission, slavery blossomed in consonance with chattelhood. Replenishment is an important concept because it was the vicious cycle through which the exploitative system was reproduced or guaranteed an appreciable supply of labor. One of the most cardinal facilitators, though, was that of appropriation, which provided masters with ill-gotten wealth at the expense of slave labor. Interestingly, this unscrupulous situation was legitimized. But before I go on to appropriation, the reader should be mindful that other laws also facilitated replenishment of labor. For instance, the phrase "personal estate" in wills and contracts included slaves. By inheritance, slave labor was perpetuated and so was the benefit. The Kentucky case of Beatley v. Judy is a case in point. Inheritance for replenishment was a serious effort to maintain continuity.[69]

Unborn children were already willed out to inheritors, as in the Banks Admr. v. Marksbury case. In this case it was decided that the owner of a female slave may give her to one of his children and subsequent issues to another.

Because slaves were personal chattel, hence property, a system of breeding slaves developed. Slaveholders would purchase female slaves and have them nursed and tended, foregoing their services during the period of gestation so that they could produce when they were fecund for the long-term benefit of the owner.

Slaves were not ranked among sentient things, and therefore generally could not marry. For the purpose of reproduction, though, it was practical to have forced marriages of slaves without sanctimony or ceremonial pomp in the obedience to their masters, whose rights to enforce such a tie was acknowledged by law. Where marriage was absent, concubinage and rape occasionally took place. The law did not recognize rape committed on a female slave as an offense.

Appropriation

Legally, the transfer of property or benefit from the slave to the master should not be construed as "appropriation." In reality, though, this transfer was actual appropriation. The masters benefitted because the slaves were legally considered chattel. However, assuming that the slaves were not chattel, the wealth amassed by masters from slaves was superfluous. Part of this wealth, in actual fact, belonged to the slave. The law was the only thing that repudiated that right.

We already have seen that the slave could possess or acquire nothing, save that which should belong to his or her master. I now will pinpoint the avenues that became open to the masters to enrich themselves because of obnoxious laws. Appropriation or expropriation should be construed as emanating from the right over property, with the slave being the property of his or her master.

The Maryland case of Hall v. Mullin established that a gift or bequest made to a slave by anyone who is not his owner would be void.[70] The courts recognized the right to dispossess slaves of property whenever there was an opportunity to do so, even in circumstances when statute law was ambiguous or silent. In the Hall case, it also was held that a slave could not make any legal contract without the consent of his or her master. This was because all sorts of benefits, pecuniary or otherwise, were directly accrued to the masters even when he or she was not supposed to be the beneficiary. Here, the masters became exploiters, deriving benefits for labor they had not expended. It was a legally parasitic ploy to become rich at the expense of slave labor. The slave's inability to make contracts was common in all British, Spanish, or French colonies.

Slaves were proxies of wealth in other respects acknowledged by law. For instance, it was legitimate either by common law or statute to gamble with slaves. This fact was upheld in the State v. Pemberton and Smith case.[71] The principle is a simple one. As Goodell points out, if the slave could possess property, he or she could dispose of it; he or she could be enabled to make contracts and, by so doing, might become a person of legal status, thereby overturning the entire fabric on which the principle of slavery was built.

Masters were given a wide range of powers to expropriate or seize unauthorized property or wealth of slaves. The authorization to gain property was of course only given to the master who was a direct beneficiary. This principle of slave property was common to most if not all the slave states, including North and South Carolina, Kentucky, Mississippi, Virginia, Tennessee, Missouri, and Maryland. In some states like Georgia, Kentucky, Tennessee, and Virginia, masters accordingly were penalized for permitting the slaves to put themselves on hire. In these instances, a convergence of interests was ensured; slavery law not only protected the interest of the masters, but when it was appropriate, it made sure that such interests did not diverge from those of the state. It is not entirely wrong, therefore, to argue that the state was an embodiment of particular interests with laws unprotecting the weak but strengthening the strong.

Concluding Remarks

The force of positive law did for American slaveholders what it did for the Roman holders of slaves. America, before the Civil War, exemplified a society in which economic conditions, specifically the use of slave labor, necessitated the provision of laws to justify the use of labor. We will recall that the arrangement of slavery struggled for legitimacy in a society that hardly was prepared by statutes to legitimize the practice. Chief Justice Mansfield's proclamation of 1772 laid the basis of English common law on the subject. The 1772 decision discountenanced the practice, but municipal law was necessary to sanction its existence. The companies bonded by colonial charter, at least in theory, could not depend on the parent country to provide a fiat for the use of slave labor. Legislation to the contrary certainly would have had dubious validity. The real test came after the Revolutionary War, when dependence on ancient culture or on *jus gentium* evolved. We are not really certain how the practice hitherto had proceeded, whether the original intention was based on indentured servitude or whether it was real slavery. One thing that is certain, though, is that after the discovery of cotton and other resources, the demand for labor to enrich a particular class of slaveholders ushered in a feverish rush to define slavery. Therefore, its real definition in America originated from economic needs of enrichment which, in reality, turned out to be exploitation.

The laws that were promulgated, or made by the courts, epitomized the extent to which positive law sacrificed natural law. The interests of the courts, the legislature, and the slaveholders intersected in the major avenues to extract profits. The laws which came into force were atavistic because a resurgence of ancient law of slavery and the way it was modified in France and Spain became effective for controlling the American slaves. Modern slavery, like ancient slavery, carried with it a severity of purpose, and like ancient slavery, collapsed because of economic and political contradictions rather than fundamental moral reasons. The declaration of status alone sufficed to acquire the required motive. All the other clarifications were mere appendages to fundamental status. Even so, the human quality of the slaves defied the simple definition, and the problem of balancing moral or natural law and positive law created some confusion.

Slaves were property. They were given qualities of inanimate objects, and as a result, this could excuse a master if he committed violence on his slaves. The very idea of criminality humanized the slaves and contradicted the declared status of slaves. Other contradictions were prevalent, but if I should focus on just one at this juncture, it would be the fact that a "property" which should make no contract ended up making contracts under extraordinary circumstances to augment the finances of the masters. Baffled as we are, positive law defined the applications of injustice in the setting of slavery. What I have done so far is to illustrate that the laws before the full-blown Industrial Revolution were inimical to the interests of the slaves or laborers. In the next three chapters I will direct much attention to conflict management, which compounded ethical issues after the Industrial Revolution. I will take a look at the judicial approach (normally confused with the state approach), and the state approach, using China as an example in the bid to implement the fundamental tenets of socialism.

Part II:

Labor Conflict Management

Judicial v. State

Chapter 4

The American Workers

Background Survey
The end of the Civil War created problems of adjustment. The demise of slavery made it imperative to substitute an alternative labor system. At first, slave cropping became a characteristic Southern way of survival as slaveholders watched with resentment the collapse of the "peculiar institution" that had provided a steady and feasible source of abundant labor. The concept of wages in the contemporary sense was remote. The working day was still prohibitively long, ten to twelve hours a day in coal pits, steel furnaces, ship building, and so on. The Industrial Revolution and the rise of big business in America catapulted the "new" order that defined later relations.

Fortuitous and manmade regulations expedited the process. A. Nevins and H.S. Commager identified six of these preconditions: 1) the availability of raw materials ("vaster and more varied than vouchsafed to any other people except possibly the Russians"); 2) inventions and techniques for converting the raw materials into manufactured products; 3) a transportation system adequate to the demands of an expanding economy; 4) a domestic market rapidly expanding with the increase in population and the growth of foreign markets; 5) a labor supply constantly renewed by immigration; 6) and the absence of adverse tariff barriers between states or sections. The protection against foreign competition and the maintenance of direct and indirect government subsidies augmented this last factor.[72]

The Revolution was based on coal, oil, iron, and eventually, electricity. That the post-Civil War years are accorded primary status does not mean the apparent dearth of inventions before them. Inventions were apparent by the end of the eighteenth century. Some of these inventions included Whitney's cotton gin, Fulton's steamboat, Howe's sewing machine and Goodyear's vulcanized rubber. But the large scale production of new appliances came with the development of the steel industry and the application of electricity to industry. F.B. Morse, one of the inventors, during the age of the new invention, worked on the principles of electrical telegraphy and persuaded Congress to subsidize the stringing of wires from Washington to Baltimore. In 1865, the Western Union Company was organized to exploit the invention. This tradition of invention extended into the twentieth century, demanding an increasing supply of labor that came from diverse sources.

Employers exploited their workers, and the visible effects can be seen in the deplorable conditions of the factories. These conditions were both physical and psychological. The psychological impediments imposed by the law were colossal, as stymied workers struggled to emancipate themselves through the formation of unions. Like the slaves and serfs of a bygone era, workers faced the antagonisms and suspicions of a judicial system that thwarted their efforts at collective action in the nineteenth century and subsequent years. To recapitulate, in my theoretical background I mentioned that all social orders have underpinnings and that these underpinnings are not usually discarded pellmell. It was not otherwise as far as the common law was concerned. At the dawn of the Industrial Revolution, the legal relationships between employers and their workers were based on agreements between the parties, on the one hand, and law and custom, on the other; the two aspects form one cohesive whole.

The Statutes of Artificers, Statutes of Laborers (which preceded it), and case law became the basis of American labor law, defined in terms of regulating contractual obligations, written or unwritten. In combination, these were a legacy from fourteenth century Britain which regulated labor in four basic ways (although in reality regulation predates the fourteenth century):

(i)   the contract clause, which prescribed punishment for abrogation of contract, meaning premature departure from contracted obligation to serve (punishable by imprisonment);

(ii)   a compulsory duty to work for those who required services when there was no visible means of support for those without jobs (the compulsory labor clause);

(iii)   service by term and not by day (particularly applicable to agricultural workers); and

(iv)   the mandatory setting of wage rates.[73]

The clarification of the master-servant relationship and the wage economy is not normally an easy one when a reconstruction of seventeenth-century England is attempted. C.B. Macpherson argues that during this period, "servant" meant the inclusion of all wage earners. Conversely, Peter Laslett and Keith Thomas argue that generally the word meant household servant. What is a common denominator for our purposes is not only that the word might have had varied usage, as R.J. Steinfeld suggests, but that it implied a superordinate and subordinate relationship authorized and legitimized by law.[74] This is the kind of conception that became relevant to the American workers of the nineteenth century. When the Statutes of Artificers and all its corollaries are tabulated and put under the microscope, the post-industrial worker was not far removed from the thirteenth-century British worker or the American slave who directly preceded this era.

In America, the epoch after the Civil War witnessed the dominance of the courts and the common law practice of regulating labor. K. Orren points out that workers had a "legal status" driven by the compulsion of industrial structure rather than contract or specific action.[75]

The compulsory labor clause of the Statutes of Artificers reappeared in America during this period. Consequently, according to Orren, if an able-bodied person without other visible means of support did not work or seek work, he could be fined or imprisoned. Two things are conjunctive here: able-bodiedness and lack of visible means of support. Together, these characteristics defined the crime of vagrancy and made it an obligation to work for masters desirous of labor input.

After slavery, the proprietary right of an individual to sell his or her labor at going market price by using his or her prerogatives was progress in notions of private property. How private this property was is questionable and open to debate, but whatever notions of privacy were enjoyed by the post-Civil War workers was dependent on their ability to prosecute a successful "industrial" confrontation with their employers. This was the avenue in which the laws became most hostile to the interest of workers, first in the courts and then with legislators. In this chapter, I will focus on (i) the wage of workers and (ii) working conditions (specifically, the length of the working day). These two factors necessitated the need for collective action, but the realization of this need became cumbersome and unobtainable.

Unions existed before 1865, since the early days of the Republic, but they had been local and weak. Unions were identifiable in the mid-1830s, and beginning in 1934, there was a first attempt at a countrywide federation of workers groups—the National Trade Union (NTU). It was about to consolidate and direct labor when it was demoralized and sent into panic in 1837. This was the result of an economic depression which sent a third of the labor force out of work and hastened the collapse of probably half of the workingmen's organizations. As the economy revived in the 1840s, though, so did the labor movement. The early labor movement addressed the length of the work day and wages; for example, the Philadelphia strike of 1834 focused on the ten-hour workday, and it involved skilled and unskilled workers.

Strategies for obtaining goals varied during this formative period, partly due to the varied sources of labor supply at a time when workers were looking for other coalescence of interests (like common ethnic background, at times common skills, and national affinity). The supply of labor came from teeming cities of Italy, Austria, Ireland, and Poland. Millions of immigrants poured into industrial cities. Most of these immigrants, combined with former slaves, were uneducated. This crop of immigrants replaced the English-speaking ones who were often members of labor organizations fighting to improve the working conditions. Because the new arrivals were often illiterate in English, communication obviously was difficult. Coal operators soon realized the unlikelihood of these workers to cement a bond of fraternity that would cripple business. Workers soon became targets of exploitation without the law. These workers often did not understand safety instructions, and they promptly became vulnerable to hazards, injuries, and death. As Congress showed little inclination to regulate private enterprise, the courts, on their part, gave substantial immunity to restrictive legislation. Not until after the turn of the twentieth century was the philosophy of "rugged individualism" effectively challenged.

The approach was confrontational with lobbying or dialogue prefacing strike actions. To this end, lobbying organizations sprouted, albeit with different techniques. The Massachusetts (1842) and the New England Workingmen's (1844), for example, attempted to coordinate efforts throughout the region. Techniques included individualistic and self-help practices involving moderation, or communitarianism of the Fourierist variety for work allocations and producers cooperatives, so that craftsmen could reap the full profit of labor.

During the post-war years, three types of labor organizations emerged: (i) the Knights of Labor (an industrial union); (ii) craft union (subsequently federated into American Federation of Labor [AFL]); and (iii) the socialist or revolutionary wing. The third group, according to Nevins and Commager, was "numerically unimportant but persistent." Farm workers, migratory workers, and domestic and white-collar workers were largely unrepresented by these groups.[76] The showdown between masters and workers commenced before the Civil War. A good number of bouts had started by the turn of the nineteenth century, bouts which witnessed the intervention of the courts and gave ascendancy to an era of injunctions.

I will now turn to the epoch which established a principle of conspiracy in 1806 that was predominant until 1895. Conspiracy did not end in 1842; actually, it barely diminished in significance.

The Era of Conspiracy: 1806-1842[77]

The courts' conception of criminal conspiracy resulted from the collective pressure exerted by workers on their fellow workers to gain concessions from their employers. Though the idea of conspiracy was enacted in various statutes, some of which were in New York (1870 and 1887) and Pennsylvania (1869-1891), one of the earliest prototypes came with the Cordwainers' case of 1806, otherwise known as Commonwealth v. Pullis.[78] The scene was Philadelphia, where a group of journeymen shoemakers went on strike for higher wages. The striking workers convinced others to join them in the strike against their masters and, by so doing, interfered with the liberty of the masters to pay whatever wages they wanted to pay. While the workers were free to strike any bargain they could with their masters, they were not free to organize collectively to force masters to pay certain wages. The doctrine of conspiracy was used extensively after the Cordwainers case to prohibit the collective organization of workers. The conspiracy cases were the law's first reaction to the growth of unions and collective bargaining.

The core of the conspiracy doctrine could be said to have originated from the common law prescriptions of master-servant law. Orren sees this arrangement as the development of American feudalism of the nineteenth century, a total system of judicial governance whereby administrative and legislative activities were carried on by judicial precepts and forms. The courts administered by injunctions, and, to a lesser extent, legislated as well as adjudicated in labor matters. The judges, Orren points out, were not forced in every circumstance to follow the common law precedent, but in the largest share of disputes that went before them, they turned to precedent and held up a structure which had existed for a long time.[79] This was one way and probably the most important trajectory of perpetuating mistakes. Theoretical mistakes, like those of the conspiracy cases, may have been perpetuated by the nature of the judicial process.

Commonwealth v. Morow, which occurred in Pennsylvania, explained the position of the common law on conspiracy. Responding to the claim that English conspiracy statutes had been received into Pennsylvania law, the judge replied that it was impractical to declare any branch of common law by statute in order to make each one commensurate with the other. The court's position was to ensure that common law was not modified or adversely changed by statute. The argument in this Pennsylvania case is that statute need not define or enforce common law to maintain a balance of the two, since the argument of the Pittsburgh Cordwainers was that English Conspiracy Statutes had not been received into Pennsylvania law.[80] This tenacity of common law assertions made it difficult, if not impossible, for statutes to be made which contradict the tenets of common law.

The doctrine of conspiracy was one important principle of lawmakers that diminished the ability of workers to act together or even come together for legal purposes. It successfully was applied in the 1830s, and together with depressions, unions fizzled. The economic recovery of the 1840s and the Commonwealth v. Hunt case of 1842 in Massachusetts revitalized the labor movement.[81] The idea of conspiracy never suffered a total blow, but the Hunt case established a significant principle.[82] It shifted liability (for refusing to work for a specific wage rate and coercing or attempting to coerce others not to work for lower wages) from criminal to civil liability as a means of controlling union activity. In the Hunt case, Leslie points out that the courts used an ends/means test to determine conspiracy so that the finding of a criminal conspiracy required proof of either an illegal purpose or the use of illegal means. After Hunt, this was the test; for example, ends/means test prevalently was used in State civil suits for injunctions.

What transpired during this early period of conspiracy? According to Wellington, workers came together to resist the downward pressures on wages. The attempt to collectively resist was pioneered mainly by skilled journeymen, who had the task of preventing others from working during a strike (scabs). It was during the strikes in these early days that criminal law was first called to intervene. The striking employees were indicted and in several cases, convicted of criminal conspiracy; this doctrine found favor with the courts in the 1880s.

Counter-Trust

The fortunes of the labor movement after the 1840s waxed and waned with prosperity and depression. The post-1840s, culminating in 1890, witnessed three important events: (i) an era of "big business"; (ii) the formation of the American Federation of Labor in December 1886; and (iii) the Sherman Anti-Trust Act (1890).

The first and third made an interesting mix that had unintended consequences for labor. Though injunctions were mainly in use during this period, the unfortunate verbiage of the Act made it feasible to talk of "conspiracy" once more. This "conspiracy" was not really intended for labor, but it came to haunt the labor movement.

Much later in the period under review, vast properties of coal, copper, iron, timber, and railroads came under the aegis of corporations. Wealth became concentrated in the hands of few, and capital was aggregated to influence policies of the state even to impinge on the direction of the national legislature. Monopolies had long been illegal in common law (as many state constitutions contained clauses prohibiting their existence). In the 1880s, more stringent laws were made and some even dissolved trusts. A trust dissolved in one state, however, incorporated in another where the laws were much more amiable or lenient with laxed enforcement. The problem then was a matter of federal rather than state regulation.

The beginning of "big business," Nevins and Commager contend, is often dated to 1882, the year that the Standard Oil Trust Agreement was drawn up. The creation of the Standard Oil monopoly inspired many other industries to consolidate into similar trusts, including linseed oil, cotton seed oil, lead, sugar, distilling, matches, tobacco, and rubber. The depression and the enactment of the Sherman Act (to be discussed later) stalled this trend in the late 1880s. When the Supreme Court took a relaxed position in the 1890s, it was business as usual, and between 1898 and 1907, the year of the "rich man's panic," companies like General Electric and U.S. Steel (the nation's first billion-dollar corporation) came into operation. This is an important development, for in later years, even until contemporary times, holders of capital influenced law makers through a coalescence of interests.

Labor, on its part, was galvanizing, and by 1869 the first important national labor organization was founded: the Noble Order of the Knights of Labor, under its first leader Uriah S. Stephens.[83] Originally meant to be a secret organization to protect its members from employers' reprisals, it eventually embraced shopkeepers, farmers and laborers. A system of worker's cooperatives was proposed to replace capitalism. The Knights embraced almost anyone who cared to join. Thus, by the late 1860s to early 1890s, a highly volatile situation existed with interests polarized into large camps of " big business" and extensive unionization. The result was confrontation and turmoil. Some of the most extensive and violent strikes occurred during this period, but in particular, those of the rail workers.

Railroad workers, having to walk to work, usually lived near the railroad center itself and rented lands owned by the railroads. Large rents often were exacted by landlords. Both coductors and locomotive engineers were paid three dollars for a twelve-hour day, and the railroad firemen received two dollars for a twelve-hour day. The brakemen had the most dangerous jobs, including racing along the narrow catwalk atop of swaying cars to spin the brake wheels on each car. This was a dangerous job that took the lives of many and made the possession of ten fingers look admirable on the job. They had neither compensation nor unions to depend on to grapple with the growing crises. Numerous railroad communities all over the country faced this situation when the president of Baltimore and Ohio Railroad announced a cut of ten percent on all wages over a dollar per day in the summer of 1877. On the day when the wage cut went into effect, there was strange calm in railroad centers, but soon trouble started at Martinsburg, Virginia, an important freight junction. Firemen abandoned their trains, and large groups of sympathizers gathered in solidarity with them. City authorities arrested the leaders of the stoppage; their friends forced their release, however, and demonstrations reached alarming proportions. At the request of railroad officials the governor of West Virginia summoned the militia, which fraternized with strikers. Two more companies of militia were sent, but with no effect. This was the strike that was to lead to a contagion of strikes Keyser, Grafton, Wheeling, Cumberland, and Newark, Ohio. In Maryland, the governor called out the national guard, and the first bloodshed took place at the Camden Station, where ten people were shot. Strikes emerged in Pennsylvania— in Pittsburgh, Altoona, Easton, Reading, Harrisburg, and Johnstown and mining districts in New York State—Rochester, Syracuse, Albany, and Buffalo; and the lakefront of Michigan—Fort Wayne, Chicago, Cincinnati, St. Louis, Cleveland. The strikes were an outcome of a combination of dissentiousness, ranging from meagre pay to discrimination in payment practices. When the smoke cleared in 1877, leaders were blacklisted, pursued by railway agents, and deprived of their jobs for years.

These strikes, not surprisingly, might have exacerbated the apprehensions of the courts, but they were equally significant for the strategies labor could use in acquiring its goals. This created controversy for workers and labor leaders.

By 1879, Powderly, the leader of the Knights, became hesitant to initiate strikes or other forms of economic pressure to gain the union's objectives. Consequently, effective control shifted to the regional leaders. A much more aggressive rank of labor was opposed to this posture. They saw hope in the railroad conflagration.

An early significant meeting of laborers in Pittsburgh (1881) was attended by some one hundred representatives of iron and steelworkers, coopers, cotton and wool spinners, cigar market, and so on. This conference resulted in the Federation of Organized Trades and Labor Unions of the United States and Canada, which was made up mostly of skilled workers. This new federation was skewed towards craft unions and developed a notion of pure wage consciousness. This organization became the American Federation of Labor (AFL) with Gompers, an immigrant cigar maker, as President.

The AFL laid the basis of the modern labor movement. Gompers believed that the organization needed to focus on the economic needs of its members in various trades and crafts. Instead of adopting the slogan of the Knights, "An injury to one is the concern of all," the Federation used as a motto "A fair day's wage for a fair day's work." The new union believed in strikes when necessary, demanded control of wealth, which was concentrated in few hands, and in its 1883 convention in Chicago, the Federation resolved that eight hours constituted a legal day's labor from May 1, 1886 and thereafter. On May 1, 1886, almost 350,000 workers took part in an eight-hour demonstration in Milwaukee, Saint Louis, Cincinnati, Washington, Baltimore, New York, Philadelphia, Boston, and other cities. In Chicago, 80,000 workers demonstrated, and as a result, about 185,000 workers immediately gained shorter workdays.

The unions clearly posed a threat to the economic interests of employers, but, as legislatures ducked, the courts continued to preside over this conflict and used whatever opportunity they had. They were given more opportunity by the Sherman Anti-Trust Act.

The Sherman Anti-Trust Act (1890)[84]

This Act, which made monopolies and other perceived impediments to commerce illegal, was used to outlaw labor unrest, more than it was to control the power of monopolies. It was the first legislation enacted by the U.S. Congress to outlaw concentrations of power that interfered with trade and reduced competition.

One of the key provisions barred every contract, combination or conspiracy in restraint of trade. "Trade" alludes to both domestic/interstate and international trade. In the Sherman Act, then, there were two important provisions: one against monopolies and another to facilitate profitable trade (domestic and international). These two provisions, which formed the core of the Act, were to be enforceable by the Department of Justice through litigation in the Federal Courts.

For more than a decade after its passage, the Act was invoked only rarely and less successfully against industrial monopolies, chiefly because of evasiveness which made narrow judicial interpretations of obstacles to trade and illegal combinations possible. What this actually paved the way for was an age of injunctions, so labor became trapped in a period of counter-trust.

Judicial Settlements and Injunctions (1893-1932)

This section shows how the courts armed themselves with the Sherman Act of 1890 and how they used it with injunctions to stifle collective action. Injunctions came into prominence during the 1870s as a result of the railroad strikes. They were the principal medium of judicial intervention in railway-labor conflicts, and they subsequently found use in major strikes and boycotts in most industries and locales. Where criminal conspiracy had been rare, anti-strike decrees became commonplace. As the number of strikes escalated, so did the number of injunctions to meet the task of pacification, which was palliated by the Sherman Act.[85]

The first application of the Sherman Act to industrial dispute occurred in New Orleans in the case of U.S. v. Working Men's Amalgamated Council (5th Circuit, 1893). The longshoremen went on strike, but the U.S. attorney was able to win an anti-strike decree under the new anti-trust law on the basis that striking unions were "a gigantic combination for the effect of restraining the commerce among several states and with foreign countries." This was a precedent for the argument that railworkers were illegally restraining trade if "they combined and conspired to quit a railroad's service with the object or intent of crippling the property or its operations."[86]

The Debs case also indicated the utility of the Sherman Act. In U.S. v. Debs (1894), the Circuit Court depended on the Sherman Law to exercise jurisdiction over labor controversies. Although the Supreme Court claimed that it relied more or less on the Interstate Commerce Act (1887) than the Sherman Act, the line of demarcation is thin.[87] Both the Sherman Act and Interstate Commerce Act were mutually compatible in the spirit of nonobstruction to trade. The Debs case arose over a dispute between the Pullman Palace Car Company and its employees and resulted in the employees leaving the service of the company. Those who were arrested, officers of the American Railway Union, were found to have obstructed the carriage of mails by combination and conspiracy.

The Pullman Palace Car Company cut wages by twenty-five percent in 1893. At Pullman, its company town near Chicago, no corresponding reduction was made in rents or other changes. This precipitated the strike of May 11, 1894, by members of the American Railway Union, following the refusal of the President, George M. Pullman, to arbitrate the dispute. The union's national council, presided over by Eugene Debs, called for a new nationwide boycott of the Pullman Cars. Sympathy strikes by union locals occurred in twenty-seven states. A morass ensued, and on July 2, partly at the request of railroad management, U.S. Attorney General Richard Olney procured an injunction from federal judges to stop the acts impeding mail service and interstate commerce. On July 4, President Grover Cleveland, acting on Olney's advice, ordered 2,500 federal troops to Chicago. The strike ended within the week, and the troops were recalled on July 20. Debs was convicted of contempt of court and conspiring against interstate commerce. It became apparent that the Sherman Act could be enforced against unions, just as injunctions could be employed to defeat action by the unions.

At this juncture, we might want to address two issues: (i) the alleged conspiracy; and (ii) the intention of the Sherman Act, at least in the eyes of one court. Judge Denman defines conspiracy in the case as "a combination of two or more persons by concerted action, to accomplish a criminal or unlawful purpose, or some purpose not in itself criminal or unlawful, by criminal or unlawful means."[88] We gain an insight into what can be seen as the ambivalence of the Sherman Act by the 1893 decision of one of the circuit courts. Did Congress make the interdiction to include combinations of labor, as well as capital? A similar decision was made in the Gompers case, where it also was held that the Sherman law covered any illegal means by which interstate commerce was restrained, whether by unlawful combinations of capital or of labor.[89] Other agents of restraint identified by the Sherman Act included unlawful contracts, trust, pooling arrangements, blacklists, boycotts, coercions, threats, and intimidation, to the extent that they be made effective in whole or in part by acts, words or printed matter.

The Danbury Hatters case (U.S. 1908) also used the Sherman fiat. In this case, otherwise known as Loewe v. Lawlor, the Supreme Court found a Sherman Act violation when a union instigated a boycott of retail stores that sold fur hats produced by a manufacturer who used scabs.[90] The defendants were members of the United Hatters of North America and the AFL, and they caused the AFL to declare a boycott against the plaintiffs to dealers in other states and against buyers who should sell fur hats.

Hence, by boycotts and strikes then, labor attempted to use its most potent weapons to come to grips with employers. It is pertinent to remember that the growth of large corporations vitiated the personal relationship between employer and employee, and that a single employee was helpless in dealing with an employer. This is the strength of unionism. Wellington puts this succinctly, saying, "industrial democracy depends upon unions, for the employee by himself is disenfranchised, if there is to be industrial democracy; decisions must be made by the employer and the representative of his employees. . . . Thus industrial democracy requires union democracy." Only by the organization of labor could workers effectively take part in determining the conditions under which they worked. It would seem that the courts were apprehensive about strikes and boycotts, which mobilized whole working-class populations; they were not restricted to particular unions or workplaces. The courts performed administrative functions and thereby became agents of what Forbath calls "government by injunctions." "Federal judges, in nearly every large city west of the Allegheny mountains—turned their courtrooms into police courts, by issuing roughly one hundred decrees prohibiting the American Railway Union (ARU) and other unions from threatening, combining or conspiring to quit in any fashion that would embarrass the railway's operations."[91]

The courts were equally incapable of solving the impasse. For instance, workers on the Denver and Rio Grande line, in receivership under the Eighth Circuit Judge, David Brewer, tested the court's offer to hear the grievances regarding intolerable working conditions. After listening to complaints, "Judge Brewer, in response, delivered a brief homily to the workers on the benevolent law of supply an demand and dismissed their claims as trivial."[92] The courts did not assume a mediating or a conciliatory role. The role of the courts during this period was exceedingly interventionist, and effectually prohibited a solution to the dispute between the employers and the employees. The cause for intervention, derived from the Sherman Act, was murky. Consequently, by the turn of the twentieth century, a strong body of opinion developed that the workers should be granted the right to organize unions without employer interference and that the employers, on their part, should be willing to acknowledge the employee unions. The United States Strike Commission, for example, criticized some of the courts and urged employers to negotiate with labor organizations.[93]

To counteract the excesses and clarify some of the ambiguities already identified under the Sherman Act, Congress enacted the Clayton Act in 1914. Some of the consequences of the Sherman Anti-Trust Act (1890) clearly were unintended. The vague language of the Sherman Act enabled large corporations to take advantage of large loopholes and engage in restrictive business that was adverse to competition. The Clayton Act (1914) was calculated to help organized labor; it even was referred to as the Magna Carta of labor. Yet like the Sherman Act, it fell short of expectations as the courts manipulated it to conform with hitherto held beliefs of pacifying labor organizations.

The Clayton Act stated that the "labor of a human being is not a commodity or article of commerce and provided further that nothing contained in the Federal anti-trust laws shall be interpreted to forbid the existence and operation of labor organizations, make the combination of members illegal or make such combinations conspiracies in restraint of trade."[94] How promptly this provision was weakened. The "Great Charter" provided marginal returns, if it made any difference at all, for the practice of issuing injunctions continued unabated. The court's intervention in labor-management relations by using the Clayton Act was a mistake. Injunctions were issued by trial courts on the basis of affidavits in *ex-parte* proceedings. Of the 118 labor injunction cases reported in the federal courts from 1901-1928, 70 were *ex-parte* restraining orders without notice to the defendants or opportunity to be heard. Because unions were weak, it was the trial court's *ex-parte* injunction that usually disposed of a case.[95] The punishment for violation of a decree was fine or imprisonment for contempt.

The 1920s saw widespread use of yellow-dog injunctions against labor actions in the Southern Coal fields.[96] During this period, the courts issued more than 2,100 anti-strike decrees. The proliferation of injunctions was met with worker obduracy of an unprecedented scale to affirm rights and liberties that have been denied them by the legal order. It soon became apparent that injunction itself was leading to industrial unrest, and that no efficient industrial order could depend on coercion to succeed. Some amount of consent was essential for labor relations. The sustenance of judge-made rules became questionable. This was the impulse to the Norris-La Guardia Act (1932), which gave federal sanction to the right of labor unions to strike or employ other forms of economic activity in dealing with management.

In February 1928, Senator George Norris, Chairman of the Senate Judiciary Committee, opened hearings on two new anti-injunction bills, and through their representatives, workers registered their diverse complaints of judicial repression.

Specifically, the law prohibited federal courts from enforcing yellow-dog contracts by restraining the issue of injunctions against; activities of labor unions. Various areas of labor activity did not warrant injunctions anymore, according to the Act, for example, organizing for union purposes, striking, refusing to work or advising others to organize or strike, and providing legal aid to persons participating in labor disputes no longer warranted injunctions.

The locus of this act is fairly discernable. Within it are two salient points: (i) the right to bargain; and (ii) judicial abstentions. Great as it was, this Act was not a panacea. Still in the limelight were other important issues. Employers still retained many self-help weapons with which to fight the establishment of collective bargaining. They legally were free to refuse to bargain, to dismiss workers (even for reasons contrived after the fact), to employ strike breakers and labor spies, or to resort to other subtle means of resistance. The inadequacy of the Act paved the way for yet another which came in 1933—the National Industry Recovery Act. The Recovery Act called on employers to guarantee rights of collective bargaining to employees without coercion. Yet for another sixty-two years, showdowns and controversies prevailed, and even today the issue is largely unresolved, with old laws, still governing modern workplaces.

From 1933 to the present, the issue in labor-management relations is how to resolve conflicts. Though controversial headways have been made, the first three decades of the twentieth century are still benchmarks for contemporary policy. Since then, there has been conflicting statutory provisions, some revisiting the Norris La-Guardia Act and showing in many respects the resilience of the courts in issuing injunctions. Other statutes have compounded the old ones, but the fundamental problem of conflicts in content persists. Post-1934 acts include the Wagner Act, the Anti-Strike breaker law, the Walsh-Healy Act, the Fair Labor Standards Act, the Taft-Hartley Act, and the Landrum-Grifin Act. Some of them are obviously well-meaning by intention. Yet some have convoluted our understanding and made the issue of reform a clarion call. The Norris-La Guardia Act, prefaced the search for an equilibrating policy.

Ambivalence and Employer Triumph (1935-Present)

Three particular acts are important for understanding this period as one of ambivalence, although allusions were made to the Sherman Act: the Wagner Act, also known as the National Labor Relations Act (1935); the Taft-Hartley Act, or the Labor Management Relation Act (1947); and the Norris-LaGuardia Act, which never died after 1935, but has been revisited by the courts in issuing injunctions though it never was intended for that purpose. This conflicting trinity has incapacitated workers and made the triumph of employers a feasibility. In this section, I shall start by taking a look at the Wagner Act.

The Wagner Act is an offshoot of the National Industrial Recovery Act (June 1933). The Great Depression was telling, and during the first administration of President F.D. Roosevelt, the Wagner Act was passed by Congress. It authorized the President to institute codes in order to eliminate unfair trade practices, reduce unemployment, establish minimum wages and maximum hours, and guarantee the right of labor to bargain collectively. The NRA, as this Act was known, faced its demise in 1935 as a result of its invalidation by the Supreme Court.

The Wagner Act, so called after its sponsor, Senator Robert F. Wagner (a New York Democrat), included a reenactment of the previously invalidated sections of the NRA and some additions. It was applicable to all firms and employees in activities dealing with interstate commerce, with some exceptions to agricultural laborers, government employees and those subject to the Railway Labor Act. It gave covered workers the right to organize and join labor movements, to choose representatives and bargain collectively, and to strike. This act also established the National Labor Relations Board (NLRB) as an independent Federal agency. [97] The NLRB was given power to determine whether a union should be certified to represent particular groups of employees, using independent methods to reach its conclusion.

The Act prohibited employers from engaging in unfair labor practices, five of which were specified:

(i.) Dominating or interfering with the formation of a labor union, including pecuniary manipulations.

(ii.) Interfering with the right of employees to organize and bargain collectively.

(iii.) Imposing preconditions for employment, such as membership or nonmembership of unions, with a clarification also guaranteeing nonunion membership or contracted workers opportunity for employment. Closed Shop and Union Shop were permitted. [98]

(iv.) Retaliation or reprisals in the form of discharge with discrimination for giving testimony or filing charges under the Act.

(v.) Refusing to bargain collectively with unions representing a company's employees.

The provisions were somewhat unfair to the employers because they set no parameters for unfair labor practices by the unions. The Act was therefore an encouragement to the growth of unionization, which actually grew by leaps and bounds. [99]

The Wagner Act acknowledged the right of workers to participate in decisions that affected their lives in the workplace; by and large, it was an essential component of social justice and democratic society. It is somewhat a paradigm for the economic essence of collective action and democracy. The basic economic idea of collective action is that workers acting collectively drive up wages, which politically provides a countervailing power to overwhelm business domination and help American democracy.[100]

The optimism espoused by the Wagner Act was buried twelve years later when the Taft-Hartley Act, otherwise referred to as the Labor Management Relations Act (1947), was passed. This Act, which was passed over the veto of President Truman, amended much of the Wagner Act and configured a phase of confusion. To some, it was a product of fear: the threat of communist infiltration into labor unions and large-scale strikes that engendered an anti-union euphoria in the United States after World War II. Sponsored by Senator R. Taft (Ohio) and F.A. Hartley (New Jersey), this Act preserved the rights of labor to organize and bargain collectively, but also guaranteed employees the right not to join unions. It outlawed closed shop, but permitted union shops where state law obliged to allow them (at times by the will of the majority of workers who desire them by voting).

According to the Act, unions were to give sixty days advance notification of a strike, and injunctions were to be granted for the length of eight days when a strike threatened national health or safety.

The Act narrowed the definition of unfair labor practices, specified unfair union practices, restricted union political contributions and required union officers, under oath, to state their position on communist affiliation. Union activities were considered unfair on several grounds, including:

• Coercion of workers who chose to bargain through representatives of their choice;

• Striking to force an employer or self-employed to join a union; and

• Secondary boycotts.[101]

• The relaxation of the Norris-La Guardia Act in order to allow injunctions against specified areas of unfair labor practice;

• Authorization of damage suits for economic losses incurred or secondary boycotts and certain strikes;

• A reorganization of the NLRB with limitations on its power;

• Authorization of suits against unions for violations of their economic interest;

• The abolition of the U.S. Conciliation Service and establishment of the Federal Mediation and Conciliables Service; and

• A prohibition on strikes against the government.[102]

Taft-Hartley, among other things, said that the government was a neutral guarantor of an employee's free choice between individual bargaining and collective bargaining. This contradicts the Wagner Act's concept of the federal government as a promoter of collective bargaining. The NLRB, then, by applying different policy "can choose between contradictory purposes and still claim they are conforming to congressional intent."[103]

69

If we should calculate a net effect, the claim that the Taft-Hartley Act did not change or erode the essential theme of collective bargaining under the Wagner Act is spurious because with Taft-Hartley, employers could resist unionization, avoid collective bargaining and even debilitate unions by financial arrangements and legal liabilities. This is significant and profound ambivalence in contemporary policy when balancing *Wagner* against *Taft-Hartley*.

Over and above the ambivalence of purpose, the triumph of employers has been well ensconced by the Taft-Hartley Act in two ways: the resurgence of judicial prominence in issuing injunctions and the replacement of striking workers.

The Norris-La Guardia Act was passed with the concept that judges were ill-equipped to pass judgment upon the social and economic disputes that would change labor-management positions or resolve the disputes. The injunctions actually protected property and the *status quo* through an interventionist method. When they were reinstated after 1947, they could not be deemed otherwise. Various cases could be cited in which injunctions were issued in the name of *Norris-La Guardia*.[104]

Three years after *Norris-La Guardia*, the Supreme Court made an important decision in the Mackay case to clarify conditions for reemployment after a strike. Strikes were given two broad characteristics: those emanating from unfair labor practices and those which were of an economic variety.[105]

In strikes over alleged unfair labor practices (for instance, the discharge of employees for union activity), workers have the right to be reinstated at the end of the worker stoppage. During economic strikes, if permanent replacements have been hired, strikers generally are entitled to reinstatement only as vacancies occur. These expectations normally are not met, and workers have been greatly disadvantaged as a result of this outcome. One of the most important objectives of collective action, which is to put economic pressure on employers, is made worthless by the ability of replacement should a protracted economic strike occur between employers and employees. This is unfortunate because production has to go on.

The million-dollar question is whether a resolution of the *Wagner-Taft-Hartley* contradiction is foreseeable in the near future. For a period of almost fifty years, the *Wagner-Taft-Hartley* contradiction has not been resolved. In some quarters, the dilemma might seem to be a necessary evil for fear of wrong intervention. Yet the recurrence of foul practices from employers and employees (but to the advantage of the employers) suggests a problem amiss.

Unfair labor practices continue to be recorded. The June 1993 Industrial Union Department (IUD) project to gather cases for affiliated unions suggests that the NLRA impedes union organizing. Hurd and Uehlein summarize some of the major problems under the following headings:

• Union avoidance routine (which involves mechanisms used by the employer to zap the formation of unions)
• Legal delays
• Blatant labor law violations (an example of which is discrimination against the leaders of union- organizing drives)
• Weaknesses of NLRB protections and penalties
• First contract problems.[106]

Employers have triumphed not only because they preside over capital (one of the means of production), but because laws have given them an uplift to gain tactical advantage and ensure continued productivity, which is obviously vital to society.

Concluding Remarks

From the borrowed robes of the fourteenth century regulation of labor in Britain, the judicial system has played a decisive role in labor-management relations, but unfortunately the judicial approach has not proved to be a panacea. The courts are, at the same time, not the best institutions to resolve this tenacious problem. Somehow, there has been a coalescence of interests between the judges and employers which makes it difficult to achieve the desired equilibrium. This is just the kind of convergence that has made the Marxist theory still attractive for a critique of the capitalist system.

The earliest interventions of the courts espoused the idea of conspiracy (until the Hunt case legally terminated what was supposed to be a criminal offense). Readers should remember that collective action was and is still the only potent tool of workers in an age when the individual is incapable of achieving his goal independently.

When in the 1890s the legislature passed the Sherman Anti-Trust Act, the courts manipulated the Act to be compliant with their traditional position. "Restraint of trade," a very broad phrase, sat well with the courts to maintain order and stability at the expense of the wishes and wants of workers. By then, there was enough cause for concern as the railway strikes caused abundant fear in the minds of all people with property. The judges had the tool to regulate labor-management relations, and they used it effectively and relentlessly. Injunctions were compounded, and with an unprepared legislature or executive branch, the judges became administrators in labor disputes. This is what Forbath calls "government by injunctions."

The motives for the injunctions were certainly cloudy in some respects. They were, however, a consistent pattern of taming "rowdy organizations." In 1932, the Norris-La Guardia Act delineated the limits of injunctions. This was a strengthening process of democracy, but even with an attempt to expunge the courts from the volatile and delicate issue of labor-management relations, the courts were skillful and resilient. Though the number of injunctions may very well have been reduced, the idea of injunctions was never extinguished. Remarkably, the courts kept a fairly consistent rhythm to challenge the presumptions of labor with no *modus vivendi*.

One could only imagine workers' relief when Congress passed the Wagner Act. Something, which like the Clayton Act should be considered a "Great Charter," but it took twelve years for the Act to be seriously jeopardized by ambivalence. The Clayton Act tried to level the playing ground, but it turned the clock backwards and invited refreshed waves of judicial interventions. At the same time the neutral guarantor of employee free choice is hardly able to prevent the excesses of abuses, (unfair labor practices, as it is called).

After 1935 the economic clout of workers waned. The epitome of worker-power, economic action, became an audacious endeavor after the Mackay case. Replacement could be swift, and nonreinstatement limitless. After all this, employers emerged as the victors. Fortuitous or incidental though the reasons may have been, the American courts played a fundamentally significant role. The challenge now is to effect a countervail for which the arguments are polarized. Some see the problem in terms of outdated laws. As Jeffrey C. McGuiness says, "[t]he 21st century is nearly upon us. Yet we are still operating under several employment laws designed for the Industrial Revolution"[107]. Those who see legislations as necessary to reverse the imbalance of power that has developed between labor and management in contract disputes are on his side. Bill Clinton used Executive Order 12866 to fight striker replacement but failed when the U.S. Court of Appeals reversed the order in 1996.

For some, the current law, as it has stood since 1938, represents a careful, working balance between the interests of employers and employees. Changing the law to deprive management of the right to replace workers would strangle many businesses, particularly smaller ones. Since attracting temporary replacements can be difficult, especially in rural areas, only a small percentage of employers use replacement workers.

Unfortunately, there is no tangible physical scale on which the interests could be weighed. It also will be disingenuous to disregard the rights of employers. But what has happened so far is the sustenance of a framework that is unfairly deadlocked. The American structure is such that the resolution of labor conflicts, irreconcilable as they are, could not be solved by the courts. I will show later on that not even the state can boast of success. History has now shown that the only probable solution would come from the reciprocal modification of demands. In the next chapter I will show how, like the American system, the British judicial system played an integral role in labor conflict that is still an unsettled problem, but which has taken a much more political dimension.

Chapter 5

The British Workers

Background Survey

Like America, Britain experienced great economic change during its Industrial Revolution. In both countries, the Industrial Revolution created the modern wage-earning class, in which the nominally free can live by selling their labor. By creating the working class, the Industrial Revolution gave birth to the labor movement as we know it. I do not presuppose here that unions and strikes did not exist earlier. Coherence and networking, which developed from a consciousness and of community, transcended the union enclaves as they existed before the Industrial Revolution.

The post-industrial era was one of uprisings in which different means and forms of organization were used against the new industrial conditions and the power of those presiding over capital. In Britain, hostility was one reaction to the advent of industrialization. This antagonism was manifestated in the revolts of the Luddites, the strikes and machine breakings of 1818, and the Chartist movement. The working class looked back with envy to its peasant days and saw the new order as one of deprivation, one in which many benefits would be extinguished, one that would bring unimagined hardships.

Like America, Britain needed to adjust. According to G.D.H. Cole, the society had to acclimatize itself to capitalism.[108] This was a period of moderation. Rather than revolt against capitalism, workers accepted industrialism as a basis of social order between 1848-1880s. Workers, therefore, revolted within the system rather than without. Trade unions and cooperative societies were built up, and workers started to send representatives to Parliament to articulate their views. The working class was embryoic, and its struggles were limited to the acquisition of better wages and conditions, the right to exist and to build its unions and cooperative societies into strong protective bodies. The struggle from within was aided by the Liberal-Labour alliance ("Lib-Lab"), which contributed to a transitional period in the growth of the working class movement.

From this period of acclimatization a socialist era arose, and when socialism became the creed of the growing body of workers, trade unionism started to appeal to the poorer and less skilled grades of workers (but labour also emerged as an independent political force). The exclusiveness of socialist influence gradually was eroded, and the idea of the working class unity found expression in both industrial and political affairs.

Like American judges, British judges are of no lesser significance, and the hostility expressed to labour organizations is correspondingly compatible at least in the formative years. The all-pervasive influence of the courts really charted the political strategy with which labourers ended up. Something that is creating considerable controversy in contemporary times as to the ability of labourers to aggregate general political interests rather than the parochial.

Trade Union as Conspiracies (1800-1824)

By the turn of the nineteenth century, the Statute of Artificers was still a familiar sight in Britain. Customary laws regulated conditions of employment, and magistrates had the power to fix wages, and the law of master and servant still existed.[109] Problems with wages and working conditions were significant during this period. Many acts, some of which were outdated or had fallen into disuse, dealt with wages and conditions in particular trades. The Spital Fields Act, for example, stipulated wages and working conditions for silk weavers. Since the theory and business of the state was to regulate wages, various trades started to band together to put pressure on the government. One of the consequences was the passage of the Arbitration Act in 1800 (amended in 1803).

During the eighteenth century, special acts were passed, usually on the petition of masters, forbidding combination in particular trades. Apart from those acts, the Judges tended increasingly to regard all workmen's combinations as criminal conspiracies under the common law.

Two general Combination Acts of 1799 and 1800 made all forms of trade unionism illegal. The Acts provided for the trial of workmen by summary jurisdiction before magistrates so that among other things, there would be expeditious proceedings against combinations. The Combination Acts sentenced workingmen who organized themselves to three months in jail or two months of hard labour. Combination and conspiracy went *in tandem* for the purpose of denying increases in wages, decreasing hours of work, soliciting support to abandon work or abandoning work with anyone else.

The sentence was to be imposed by two magistrates, and appeal was made extremely difficult. In addition, anyone contributing to the expenses of a person convicted under the Act was subject to a fine. The illegitimacy of combinations was directed not only against employees, but against employers as well. However, there is no recorded case of the law ever being enforced against employers.

The economic activities of workers clearly hastened the promulgation of these laws. Though the mutiny at Nore and the rebellion of the United Irishmen prompted the new measures, there were other, greater concerns to be sought in the organization of miners and factory workers in the Northern and Midland countries. The leadership of intelligent artisans particularly was dangerous for the rapid proliferation of discontent, which would fuel an explosive situation in the mines and factories, where conditions were deplorable. The Combination Acts, then should be construed as unmistakable instruments to suppress the working-class movement. Until about 1808, they were successful to the extent that no stable working class combinations arose in the factories of the mining districts.[110] In addition, strikes and riots were localized.

In 1805, the weavers formed a general combination to pressure Parliament into passing a minimum wage act, but this bill was overwhelmingly defeated in the House of Commons (HOC) in 1808. The inability of the government to respond, provoked strikes in defiance of the Combination Laws. The strikers included cotton and woolen weavers in Lancashire; miners in North Umberland (1810) over yearly bond issues; and the weavers in Scotland (1812). This strike led the magistrates to fix a scale of payment, and went on for about three weeks until authorities arrested the strike committee and charged the members with conspiracy.[111] Although the Combination Acts did not extend to Scotland, the Scottish judges also regarded combination in itself as an offense.

The punishment was imprisonment from four to eighteen months. After the strike was broken, the union shattered. The workers denounced this as injustice, but there was no cohesive force among workers or parliamentary radicals for the abrogation of the Combination Laws. It would take a combination of Francis Place, Joseph Hume, J. McCulloch, and the Benthamites to formidably challenge the Combination Act and get it repealed.

Wages and hours were two serious problems during this period. At first, wages were separately negotiated for each town, but gradually, uniform price lists extending over a wider area were developed, and wages were adjusted by making uniform percentage additions or deductions to or from the list. As a result, prices grew. Wage negotiations were simplified, and as bargaining on wage issues became centralized, the power of amalgamation simultaneously grew.

During this period, workers attempted to get lawmakers to pass laws that would be sympathetic to the interests of workers. This was impossible, partly because of the very complexion of Parliament. There was limited franchise in the counties and boroughs, which excluded the new industrialist classes. It was not until 1832 that the first attempt was made to transfer voting privileges from small boroughs dominated by nobility and gentry to the heavily populated industrial towns. This attempt did not even adequately meet the task at hand.[112]

The major obstacle was the position of the law on conspiracies, which made trade unions illegal during the first quarter of the century. The courts held them to be criminal conspiracies in restraint of trade at common law, and they were made expressly illegal by the Combination Acts. In addition, under the Unlawful Societies Act (1799), regional or national unions were declared illegal. Master-Servant laws also challenged the compliance with union decisions. The enforcement of the combination and conspiracy laws had been rigorous and repressive. It was not until the 1820s that a lapse in intolerance set in. This was partly due to ownership of property which did much to alleviate the distress for manufacturing districts and allayed some of the fears of employers as panic subsided and tolerance began; the power of middle-class radicalism was directed largely to the mobilization of public opinion, which increased. The state perceived reform as contending, but safe, comparison to revolution. This spirit greatly facilitated the repeal of the combination laws (promoted through Francis Place and others). Contrary to the expectations of these architects, the repeal gave a *carte blanche* incentive to organize and strike. The repeal was not an agent of diminution, but a catalyst of exacerbation. Between 1824 and 1825, strikes mounted in many occupations, especially that of the textile workers in Scotland.

Alarmed employers pressed the government for a repeal of the 1824 Act. What was the 1824 Act, anyway? It was not a *carte blanche* for instability; it barely granted immunity against prosecution under the Combination Act and conspiratorial prosecution under common law. Combinations merely were legalized for dealing with questions of wages and hours. Penalties against intimidation, molestation or obstruction, and against attempts to coerce either employers or fellow workers into submission of worker interests surrounded the new concession that was granted to workers. Although it still was legal to form trade unions, they were to be formed under extraordinarily precautionary circumstances so that penalties under statute or common law were not incurred. This calculated ambivalence made nonsense of the repeal.

Hence, after 1825, workers were prosecuted for virtually the same offenses while the combination laws were in force. Like the Commonwealth v. Hunt case in America, the repeal of the Combination Acts relieved workers of criminal liability of merely organizing themselves. There was an additional marginal benefit for the British workers; they could maintain an open and continuous existence of trade unions for some years immediately after 1824. The foundation was laid for openly constituted trade unions in a large number of trades.[113]

The Epoch of Dilemma (1825-1875)

This period in British legal history is a mish-mash of confusion, for which the ability of workers to re-organize was not clearly defined. It witnessed the repeal of Combination laws; the Master-Servant laws (of ancient antiquity); the Hornby v. Close case (1867); the Chartist movement; strikes over hours of work; the Conciliation and Arbitration Act; and finally, the Labour Laws of 1875, which partly came from agitation to repeal the Criminal Amendment Act.

A cursory look at the combination of these laws and cases gives us an intuition of ambiguity and confusion. Two of the lot are particularly striking: the Master-Servant laws and the repeal of the Combination Acts. The need to resolve the problem probably started in 1864, when Trade Unions began their concerted campaign for the amendment of the Master-Servant Acts.

The Master-Servant laws were repugnant, if not in their entirety, for two things: (i) they obligated workers to work for a specific period to one employer without giving them any guarantee of permanent employment; and (ii) the conditions for a breach of this contract were extensive and included premature departure from work. Premature departure from work or any form of stoppage made workers criminally liable. This contradicts the spirit and intention of the 1824 Act, which repealed Combination.

In the 1840s, the Master-Servant laws were used to repress strike action and vitiate the formation of unions. Trade unions suffered greatly during this period, particularly so when they were also in their burgeoning stage; this may be seen with the Miner's Association of Great Britain. Strikes in the Northern Countries, South Wales, and those organized by the West Yorkshire and Durham Miners suffered frustrating setbacks. G.D.H. Cole points out that more than any other body of workers, "the miners were faced with continued legal repression," which was necessitated by the purpose of keeping the Master-Servant laws intact.[114]

Clearly, the makers of law were less receptive to the complaints of the working class, and from this early point in time, the strategy to achieve the goal of workers became a political one. For this reason, it diverged from the confrontational style that was prevalent in America.

I shall begin to substantiate the political argument by looking at the Chartist movement. The Chartist movement itself could be traced back to 1838, when William Lovett founded the London Workingmen's Association (LWMA). In May of that year, the LWMA published what came to be known as the People's Charter. Six demands were prominent:

- annual parliaments;
- universal male suffrage;
- equal electoral districts;

- end of property qualification;
- payment of members; and
- secret ballot.

When scrutinized closely, this was a working-class movement with political demands. It would seem that the perception of workers was that the solution to workers' problems inherently depended on the political makeup of Parliament. To impress on the law makers the seriousness of workers' demands, militancy was used. There were riots in 1839, 1842, and 1848, all launched at a time of great economic distress. Notwithstanding the riots, the Chartist movement failed for a combination of reasons, but largely because it was not connected with either the middle class or the lower class. The movement was not a total failure, however; it was a sensitizing advocate from which workers drew inspiration for later successes as all six points were secured with the exception of annual parliaments.

The tradition of protest against economic returns for labour continued even after the Chartist debacle. But the law was less sympathetic at each turn to the cries of the working class. In 1853 for instance, the Preston Spinners went on strike for advance in wages. Employers retaliated with a general lockout.[115] Manufacturers throughout the Lancashire region collaborated, and scabs or blacklegs were imported. The leaders of the strike were arrested, kept without trial, and driven back to work.

By the 1850s, it was apparent that the Master-Servant laws and the Statute of Artificers were an impediment to workers' interests. In the 1860s workers tried to overturn these laws, but they had no success either with Parliament or the courts. In 1864, Alexander Campbell, leader of the Glasgow Trades Council, pioneered the attack on laws which had been inactive for a protracted period since their enactments. Three years later, notwithstanding attempts to repudiate it, the Master-Servant Act became law. It however narrowed disparities between the master and his servant for a breach of contract. There was an uneasy balance between summary arrests and the powers granted to magistrates to arrest workers before a trial. The ability of employers to effect a lock out remained unresolved, and this was detrimental to workers. During this stalemate, two of the most important events in British labour history evolved: "Sheffield outrages" and the Hornby v. Close case in 1867.

The "Sheffield outrages" were acts of violence against scabs, which became significantly explosive in the late 1860s and necessitated government intervention. The Trade Union Commission Act, which set up a Royal Commission to investigate and make reports on the organization and rules of trades and other associations, resulted from the outrages. The Commission had the power to investigate acts of "intimidation, outrage or alleged wrong to have been promoted or connived" by trade unions and other associations. The vehemence with which the Sheffield outrages were conducted by workers created extreme union resentment, similar to the railway strike of the 1870s in America.

In the midst of controversy, the Court of the Queen's Bench handed down a decision in the Hornby Case that unions were in restraint of trade, and because they were illegal associations they could not claim protection for their funds against defaulting officers. This decision had two significant effects: (i) the lack of protection of union funds; and (ii) the outlawing of trade unions. Henceforth, the thrust was toward Parliamentary agitation.[116]

From 1825 to 1875, therefore, trade unions were of dubious legality. They were not recognized by the law, although the Combination Acts had been repealed. The injustice I have alluded to in the introduction continued, for which the experiment in collective action became even more essential. Between 1869 and 1870, trades revived.

The number of strikes and complaints about nine hours of work increased, and the government was brought closer and closer into the drama. In America, the attempt to resolve laws by the federal government came in 1938 with the Fair Labour Standards Act, which established minimum wages and maximum hours for all workers engaged in covered interstate commerce. The intensity and tenacity of the nine-hour movement fell on the deaf ears of lawmakers, and when the bill was introduced in the House of Commons (HOC), liberals voted against it on principles of *laissez faire*. Lengthy hours of work affected many and depended largely on the Act of 1850 (sixty hours a week). The intransigence of liberals was cumulative. Not only did the Liberals cripple the attempt to reduce working hours, but they also ardently supported the Criminal Amendment Act of 1871. The Act itself stifled the ability of workers to obtain a voluntarist solution.[117] When the liberals fell in 1874 because of their cumulative intransigence over workers' interests, the workers were able to gain marginal success one more time in 1875.

The Labour Laws of 1875 supported workers' collective action but in Britain, like America, the courts played a significant role in frustrating the working-class movement.[118] As many focus their attention on one group of lawmakers, it also may be pertinent to focus on the vigor with which the courts could vitiate the intended spirit of laws when the laws are ambivalent. In Britain, the Taff Vale case, at the turn of the twentieth century, illustrates this. Until the Taff Vale, what was one of the greatest legal conundrums (the right to collective action) seemed settled by the Laws of 1875. This was no longer the claim after 1900.

Court Intervention and the Labour Party (1876-Present)

After 1876, British courts continued to extend less conciliatory settlements in labor disputes. As workers became even more frustrated with the making of laws and their interpretation, they hastily sought a political approach to negate the inimical attitude confronting them. By so doing they inadvertently dragged society into labor conflicts, for no political party could capture political power without selling an agenda that will be acceptable to the larger section of society. This is the problem that has come to taunt the Labour Party. I will focus on the incapacity of the Labour Party to obtain a political solution,but this should be construed as a derivative of judicial distrust. Yet another way to confront the issue is to analyze the extent to which the agenda of the party could be all-embracing with very little or no strings attached to the unions which brought it into existence over ninety years ago. This problem has evolved from the basis that brought the party into existence. The party was a political expedient to circumvent judicial phobia of the nineteenth and early twentieth centuries. Whether the lawmakers of the nineteenth century could be exculpated in all this is subject to controversy, but to understand the crisis of the union today vis-a-vis the party, I will focus on three aspects: (i) the 1876 Trade Union Act; (ii) the Taff Vale case; and (iii) the Osborne Judgment.

Readers should recall that the Trade Union Acts of 1871-1876 withheld the rights and responsibilities of incorporation from trade unions. The Acts also legalized the existence of trade unions and a number of activities essential to their effective conduct. It largely was presupposed that the unions had immunities against suits in courts of law by their registered names, or in any way for a wrong not explicitly mentioned in the statutes.[119]

Large numbers of unincorporated associations developed, performing important acts and owning substantial property as a result of the deprived rights of incorporation. In answer to the problems that arose over nonincorporation, a judicial theory of representative action arose, whereby the incorporated could sue or be sued in the name of one or more of its officers or members on behalf of the entire membership. This theory played a vital role in truncating the efficacy of trade unions until 1906, when it was nullified by the Trade Dispute Act. The tug of war in the Taff Vale case was arguably between a presumption of law and a judicial theory. But it is pertinent to remember that judicial rulings are never a solution to the intrinsic problem in labour-management relations. What really happened in the Taff Vale case?[120]

The Taff Vale Railway Company brought a suit against the Amalgamated Society of Railway Servants (ASRS). In August of 1900, members of the ASRS went on strike for higher wages and union recognition, but settled within a fortnight when the company employed blacklegs. During the strike, the company began legal actions against the union, complaining that picketing violated the Conspiracy and Protection of Property Act (1875).

The ASRS, for its part, held that because it was neither a corporation nor an individual, it could not be held liable. The court of Justice Sir George

Frarwell decided that a union could be fined for damages caused by the actions of its officials in individual disputes. The House of Lords (HOL) upheld this decision, and charged the ASRS £50,000.[121] This decision was important for employers. As H.A. Cleg and others state, "[h]ad British employers wished to be rid of trade unions, the depression years of 1902-5, with the Taff Vale precedent valid in every court were as favorable an opportunity as ever presented itself."[122]

The Taff Vale verdict eliminated strike as a weapon of organized labour for which an alternative was necessary. To overcome the fiasco of judicial decision, workers rushed to a political strategy, a mechanism of grabbing the bull by the horns. Their intention was to circumvent and countervail the hostility of judicial interventions they had witnessed for several generations. This led to the formation of the Labour Party in 1906.

The Labour Party first came forth in 1900 as the Labour Representative Committee and then as the Labour Party in 1906. It was apparent to workers that no strike would be safe, except a purely unofficial movement ironically conducted with no organization behind it to rewrite judge-made law. The nascent party seemed strategic because between 1900 and 1906 the number of labour leaders to Parliament rose from two to twenty-nine, but more importantly, the Taff Vale judgment was negated by the Trade Disputes Act of 1906. The start of the twentieth century was a period of close alliance between liberals and labourers as the repudiation of Taff Vale shows. The union of the Labour Party and the liberals resulted in the famous "Lib-lab" collaboration.

Not too long after Taff Vale, however, the test of this collaboration came to the limelight over the Osborne case. The main question here is whether the lawmakers in Parliament could ensure the interests of the working class. The chain of events started when W.V. Osborne, one of the branch secretaries of the ASRS, brought a suit against the ASRS to restrain it from a form of expenditure he maintained was ultra-vires, expenditure which, in effect, was to support the Labour Party.

Trade unions had been using their funds for political agitation since the early 1860s and, equally, to promote trade union candidatures since the Reform Act of 1867. From 1903, in order to establish a common discipline, the Labour Party required from its candidates a pledge of loyalty in the constitution and the decisions of the Party. In the Osborne case, a problem arose over the defining clause of the 1876 Trade Union Act, which enumerated all the activities the unions could perform, except subsidiaries that were considered legal. All other forms of activities were, by inference, illegal or ultra-vires declarations. Trade unions thus were treated as corporate bodies, not owing their existence and power to statute law. Though legislatures side-stepped this consideration in 1871, 1876, and 1906, it haunted them after 1909 because of the Osborne judgment.

The December 21, 1909, judgment vindicated Osborne, and the unions were left to scramble once again over the fundamental basis for financial support. The unions, which the judges saw as corporations or quasi-corporations, had to find a way to reverse this judgment by fresh legislation, just as they had done in the Taff Vale, particularly, because one thing was troubling—starvation, which would inevitably come from the lack of income. Injunction after injunction prohibited large, affiliated trade unions from contributing financially to the Labour Party, and by 1910, the adverse effects became apparent as the number of labour candidates dwindled. The fate of workers then came to rest on lawmakers in Parliament. In retrospect, some looked to the Taff Vale case as a benchmark of glory, an experience that should help the overturn of Osborne. In reality, though, this was somewhat disingenous for a number of reasons.[123] Within the unions, disagreements occurred that conflicted with profound liberal precepts. Some members refused to accept a partial reversal of the judgment because of what they perceived as the intrusion of government into union affairs. The clash of interest, to start with, was predicated on the liberal insistence to uphold a principle of faith in individual conscience and minority rights. Whereas some labour leaders gave a retaliatory torpedo blow on the judgment by disallowing dissenters a right to opt out of political fund contributions, after a protracted battle, a partial reversal was obtained in 1913 that granted trade unions the unrestricted right to opt out of payment to union political funds.

By 1911 the Party had a foretaste of the problem of embracing the ideas and aspirations of trade unions wholeheartedly and aggregating the general interests of society. This was a difficult balance to maintain later on, particularly since the hold of unions over the Party was very pervasive in the 1980s. This is evident, at least, in the following ways: (i) the union's role in the electoral college for the leader and deputy leader; and (ii) the union's role in the selection of Parliamentary candidates.[124]

In the 1990s the diminution of this link still has been affected. We know that two camps, which should be observed with some precautions—modernisers and traditionalists—have somewhat polarized the Party and aided our understanding of the party-union links. Modernizers like Tony Blair favor fundamental reforms while traditionists resist or contend against such reforms in many, if not all, respects. But even as the tug of war goes on, the Party, like the unions, need each other. The financial support of the Party derived from the unions is substantial. In 1993, for example, Labour gained £4.7M out of a national income of £8.8M in 1993, from unions.[125]

But let us jump back to the crux. We need to zero in on the efficacy of political action and ask a fundamental question. Have the workers found haven in what they created? If not, why not? The political parties now have many problems to arbitrate and many factions to integrate. Like the

Tories, Labour is concerned about rising costs, increasing inflation and jobs. The greatest challenge now for Labour is not only to fight against what workers would perceive as exploitation and poverty, but balancing the interests of the owners of the means of production and that of the employed and the unemployed. This is because the success of the party in capturing political power does not entirely depend on the trade unions, but on the way in which the general public perceive the intentions of Labour. Therefore, within Labour itself, we see a system of checks and balances, evolving in a way that Labour must first and foremost check the ambitious designs of the Trade Union Congress (TUC) against the general expectations of the public. This is an unintended consequence of having the political party. But who would not have expected this consequence in the long-run, knowing the nature of political parties. How effectively this contentious alliance will secure the working class interests in years to come is unknown. What is known is the predictable force of the law when labour crises ensue to create a political and economic morass.

However, by shifting the emphasis from voluntarism to political strategy, the British workers have made one gallant leap toward breaking loose of the legal trepidations that have harangued them in bygone years. It seems to me that the problem they are confronted with now is not the intransigence of law per se, but, ironically, the formation of alliances in a political environment to challenge and make laws that will fit them when the need arises. When the potential is great to form the needed alliances, amiable laws could be made. Societal consideration now works as a countervail to what might be the overambitious proclivities of workers. The issue of commensurateness or fairness is somewhat catching on in the political arena. Modernizers are also significantly gaining the edge as evinced by the success of Tony Blair to the premiership in 1997.

Concluding Remarks

Like American workers, British workers have been uneasy with labour law, not only because of the manner in which laws have been created, but in the way the courts have interpreted them. The struggle of the working-class movement in Britain has been a protracted one. Laws with dual intentions characterized the process, prescribing conspiratorial and criminal acts, and sometimes affirming the legitimacy of unions. This suggests one more time how positive law can flip-flop to gain some moral grounds.

Unrestrained suppression of the labour movement was supposed to have lasted legally until 1824. But in 1825, when the Combination Act was repealed, an era of ambivalence was opened. Organized workers held a confused status.

Workers were legally or nominally permitted to organize within restricted parameters. The Master-Servant laws were still intact for the greater part of the nineteenth century, and they made concessions to workers suspect. By their very nature, Master-Servant laws made strikes illegal. To break free of bondage, workers directed their anxiety against lawmakers. Militancy culminated in the Chartist movement which made strange political demands for an economic problem.

The 1860s resonated the incapacity of lawmakers to empathize with the working-class movement or to sanction fully the legitimacy of trade unions. The intransigence of the courts' was persistent, and the decision in the Hornby case, which held trade unions in restraint of trade portrayed a significant lack of protection of union funds. An extension of intolerance also was manifested in the deprivation of rights to form unions. This contradicted the spirit of the Anti-Combination Laws of 1825. Fifty years later, when the trade unions were granted at least a modicum of legal status, it did not take long for the courts to divest them of the cloak of benefit. This was the exemplary Taff-Vale case. The case jolted trade unions to form a political party to counteract hostile judicial decisions.

The success which the workers achieved after the Taff-Vale case was a source of inspiration and strength. The inspiration, however, was premature and nonsustainable. The problem came with Osborne, which brought into sharper focus the essentiality of political alliance in achieving the goals of Labour, so that the political expedient defined by Taff-Vale was a tactful, but not a flawless variety. To perform the political functions required of a political party, parochialism becomes problematic. The task of Labour now is how to get around this parochialism that catapulted it into a political party with trade unions caught in the middle of the conundrum. This issue helped polarize the party into traditionalists and modernizers, labels that should be used with some precaution. They, in actual fact, attempted to define the relationship of trade unions to the Labour Party by the extent to which union severance or detachment should be made from the party. This has clouded the original intention of creating the party and many now wonder whether the party in its traditional form is demoded. The question is whether the bond is good enough to acquire the maximum expectations of workers. The answer is unknown insofar as millions of interests are now involved. Thus, applauding the political solution is controversial. One thing is certain—the success of British workers is no longer the product of an isolated effort (meaning concerted unionization). This is so on two grounds:

(i)   to make laws that will empower the workers, such laws will have to be arbitrated against the wider interests of society because Labour will have to secure extra political support containing "foreign" interests; and

(ii)   to repudiate or reverse any decision of the House of Lords using Parliamentary legislation, the same procedure will have to hold.

Britain provides an interesting development in conflict management. Not only is the judiciary significant, but unlike America, a political party with a largely labour agenda ensued from the labour crisis to countervail judicial distrust. It is, however, more apparent now than ever that Labour by itself cannot go it alone. It needs helpers and therefore flexibility in its goals. This is the focus of "new labour" under Tony Blair. Chapter Six focuses on the response to both the judicial and legislative failures in both America and Britain.

Chapter 6

The Chinese Workers

A Case Study of the *Proletarian State*

In America and Britain, we already have seen some of the drawbacks of law making and the judicial attempts to resolve labor conflicts in liberal democratic societies. I did not presuppose that all labor laws are unjust, because the truism is that there are certain moral justification for virtually all positive laws, and attempts are normally made to inject notions of morality into them through some interpretations given by courts.

The Chinese situation is more or less a response to the failure of the judicial approach to conflict management. In China the state assumes full responsibility by the use of ideology and the implements of coercion to manage labor relations.

The *proletarian* state cannot be extricated from labor management in China, because by autonomy in domestic and foreign relations, *state* power has been used to ascertain that the welfare of the workers will be paramount. The state is thus the trust fund of the workers to manage their affairs by domestic and external policies. This is why for example, for so many years the Chinese government was opposed to Free Trade as a matter of foreign policy. This "unconscionable freedom" it is perceived, fails to protect workers, and provides fresh fields for the exploitation of wage-labor. China restricted trade, formed an alliance with Russia, and several Sino-Soviet joint stock companies emerged.

The Chinese experience itself made it propitious and easy to reject notions of Free Trade. Foreign domination brought to China a substantial amount of the evils associated with industrial capitalism, and capitalism in China was closely linked to imperialism. The national bourgeoisie was dragged into the orbit of capitalism by imperialism.

There are always three component issues to be addressed in labor conflict management: (i) labor and wages; (ii) capital and profit; and (iii) increased productivity at minimum cost for societal benefit.

The concept of the proletarian state is a problematic one, because it presupposes a state infused with workers' interests, from which the interests of society could subsequently be realized. This was the basis of the Maoist proletarian state which fell into serious difficulties in the attempt to epitomize the working class movement. Balancing the interests of workers and that of society leaves us with two propositions: (i) widespread employment, long hours of work and meager wages; and (ii) production at minimum cost to increase wealth, which is also the goal of the capitalist. If proposition one holds, the essence of the working class is lost, since long hours and meagre wages define a concept of injustice that caused it to revolt in the first place. We therefore have reaction with state ownership of the means of production, suggesting that the interest of the workers has not been maximized.

Incidentally this is so because the second proposition is directly related to the first. Wages are part of the cost of production, and one reason for keeping them low is to derive profit or economic profit, which is necessary to increase investment. This reality was the first challenge of the Maoist proletarian state.

The Maoist *Proletarian State* (1948-1977)[126]

Marx and Engels were particularly concerned about two main classes, the proletariat (those who own no means of production and could only sell their labor for wages), and the capitalist (those who exploit wage-labor). The peasants were considered a "dangerous class" and were given a substandard role in the working class revolution. Their lack of consciousness made them incomparable to the proletariat. However, in China of the 1940s, this insignificant mass of men gave new meaning to the supporters of the Marxist revolution, one of them being Mao, who came to exemplify one of the towers of neo-Marxist thought. Little did Marxist realize that a theory meant for the urban working class of advanced industrialized nations, would become a paradigm for an anticapitalist peasant country.

The goal set by Mao for the Chinese people was essentially to fend off imperialism, based on the concept of *perceptual* and *rational* knowledge. This means that China's destiny will be shaped by what it saw of the internal and external contradictions of imperialism, as well as its perception of the motive of oppression and exploitation wrought by imperialism in collaboration with China's comprador and feudal classes.

The attainment of economic justice depended on the proletarianization of the peasants, and movement of economic activities from the already corrupted urban areas to the rural areas, where communes should be created. This conformed with the ambitious designs of the Great Leap, which was an attempt to decentralize economic and political life in relatively autonomous and self-sufficient rural communes.

With the 1948 victory of the Chinese Communist Party (CCP), which was made propitious by a peasant revolt over urban dwellers, Mao started his objectives for the creation of a socialist society. His dictatorship was legitimized by the authoritative legal statement of the 1949 Organic Law for the Chinese People's Political Consultative Conference.

Maoism is founded on the idea that "labor is the foundation on which human society exists and develops," and that "workers are the creators of civilization."[127] He even described the workers as the "most far-sighted, just, and unselfish [people] endowed with revolutionary thoroughness."[128]

To rectify the economic injustice caused by imperialism, the state became instrumental in many ways. Many confiscations were reckoned in the formative years of the proletarian state, particularly property of the nationalists. One of the major intentions of the state was to zap the system of bureaucratic capitalism. The assets came in varied forms: industries, railways, real estate, and military supplies, to name a few.

Between 1949 and 1952, the state started his attack on the feudal landlords. According to the Land Reform Law of June 28, 1950, land draft animals, farm implements, surplus grain and surplus housing of landlords were to be confiscated. The Land Reform Law was an attempt to redistribute land, which is a major source of wealth in a feudal economy. By its confiscations and antagonism, the state created no incentive for capital savings.

Notwithstanding the leading class role in society, the workers were to accept the leadership of the Communist Party. The struggle which ensued between the Communist Party and the workers indicate that labor conflicts cannot be trivialized, but more so, that the state could be ill-equipped to deal with the problems of workers or articulate the interests of the working class.

The state became ambivalent by trying to exalt the position of the working class in Chinese society, while at the same time strengthening the Communist Party and its control over the workers. Conflict management in this proletarian state was orchestrated by the government.[129] Matters concerning wage level and profit margin were first discussed by direct negotiation between capital and labor, but the final settlement of such matters was made by the government. Once the government decides objections are characterized as contrary to the will of the people.

The concept of the people is a controversial one that focuses on the utilitarian assumptions of rights, not necessarily of the classical variety, which attempts to embrace both moral and legal rights. Here there is some kind of resolve to harmonize individual rights with collective rights, and therefore vouch for their interdependence.[130] This notion of rights is what carried with it repercussions for trade unions and workers in the Maoist state.

Though trade unions have a long history in China, they are essentially vehicles for the control of labor and capital by the government. On June 28, 1950, the Government Administrative Council (GAC), adopted The Trade Union Law of the People's Republic of China.[131] Article 9 of this law made it imperative for unions to fall under striking compulsion to support the decrees of the government, and to oppose acts in violation of government laws and decrees which are detrimental to production. By so doing the government encouraged a practice of democratic centralism, which made trade unions a union of representatives (selected by the government), rather than a union of workers. Democratic centralism supported the idea that the minority must submit to the will of the majority. Discussion of an issue ceases once a decision has been rendered, and all trade unions must accept the decisions and directives of the All China Federation of Labor.

All unions in China are to be examined and approved by the ACFL or its affiliates before they can be registered. Nonconformity to the constitution of the ACFL and the trade union law prohibits the freedom or the right to organize a trade union.

The welfare of the Maoist workers depended largely on the general state of economic performance. Hence, declining performance went in tandem with declining living conditions and wages. Wages are a matter of interpretation in the proletarian state. For the worker, it is the remuneration for his labor; to the individual employer, it is that portion he pays his employees as part of his total cost; and for the national economy, the aggregate consumer purchasing power.

From its earliest beginnings the proletarian state was opposed to increased wages. The policy of increasing wages was seen as an ultra-left, welfare-of-the-toilers policy that did not take into consideration public and private interests and benefits to both labor and capital. If the state was predicated on the idea of the harmonization of interests, its scheme was too ambitious and contradictory. What in actual fact, the state went on to endorse was the division and polarization of interests. It made known the following facts: (i) high wages is tantamount to high costs to manufactures, which will suffocate increased productivity; (ii) high wages cannot heighten the political consciousness of the workers; and (iii) high wages will sensitize the passions of the peasants and exacerbate conflict between workers and peasants.[132]

During the formative years of the proletarian state, the state adopted measures to placate the workers by bringing the rate of unemployment down. For example, there was to be no dismissal of workers without the prior permission of the Bureau of Labor.[133] But there was a group of workers who were unaccounted for, and who sustained the proletarian state for its duration. These humans enabled the state to compete with private enterprises, and obtain no direct rewards for their labor. These workers who were mainly prisoners, and adversaries of the system, worked on farms, and built roads and bridges without pay. Labor was intensive on these farms and conducted under the illusion that output will increase per unit of land. The state clearly did not restore the dignity of labor. What it really succeeded in doing was reducing cost for risky projects undertaken not only in agriculture, but other public enterprises at the expense of natural rights, the violation of which means something to the moralist, but little or nothing to the utilitarian.

The Maoist state therefore utilized labor to realize some results by sacrificing some of the individual tenets of the Marxist concept—short hours, adequate payment, and economic justice. Inflation was stabilized after the turbulent Kuomintang (KMT) years, living standards of the poorest peasants increased, and unemployment fell in the cities.[134] Yet it will take about eighteen years after the fall of the classical proletarian state to grant the Chinese workers some legal rights in matters of wages and employment. The concept of minimum wage was placed in the CCP's agenda since 1948, but it was never legislated or implemented.[135] The classical proletarian state expired with Mao in 1976 without ascribing any judicious or legal rights to the working class movement.

The Reformed *Proletarian State* (1978-Present)

After Mao's death concepts of modernization challenge some of the preconceived notions of his proletarian state. Bureaucrats tip-toed on the issue of class conflicts, moved towards market socialism and distanced themselves from much of Mao's revolutionary Marxism. But neither Mao nor his heirs could set China on a consistent course.

Issues which were once considered to protect the working class and jobs, like protective trade, began to give way to market socialism. The primary objective was to transform the highly centralized operational system to increase trade in a way suitable to the open economy. By 1985 the number of foreign investments enterprises and the amount of foreign investment have more than doubled, while the individual and private economy has increased by leaps and bounds.

The number of private enterprises in major cities like Shangai developed from zero to 7,600 in 1994.[136] All along Shangai had struggled to break down the monopoly of state-owned and collective industrial and commercial enterprises.

The Fourteenth National Congress of the Communist Party of China (CPC) convened in September 1992, and introduced the establishment of a socialist market economy as the goal of reform. This precedent necessitated an amendment of the CPC constitution.

The amended constitution provided some benefits for the workers. For example, wages went up and some legal rights were achieved. Yet the workers have not found a panacea in the reformed state. One major problem for the reformed state is putting the concept of market socialism in perspective. This confusion is highlighted by many, including A. Przeworski, who suggests that "If market socialism is a system that legislates against only a few property and allocates most resources using markets, then it is identical with capitalism, [but] if... it is to be a distinct system, it must legally discriminate in favor of worker-owned cooperatives. . . . "[137] In the *Beijing Review*, Li Lanqing defines a Chinese perception of the socialist market economy as "a structure wherein public ownership plays a dominant role and various economic sectors enjoy common development."[138]

The obstacles confronting the workers in the post Maoist state were enormous. For example unmarketable products, outdated technology, and redundant personnel. These factors and more, coupled with reforms became good recipe for the June 1989 Tiananmen conflagration and labor strikes. The strikes show what was hidden but latent in the classical state. By 1988-89, price inflation had gotten to 30 percent, with state workers lagging behind in wages.[139] Not even sections of the army could be trusted to quell rebellion. Not surprisingly, by the turn of the 1990s it became crucially necessary to address the plight of the workers once more.

Minimum Wage and Labor Law (1989-Present)

Although the minimum wage has been on the agenda of the Communist Party since 1948, it never materialized as an issue.[140] Minimum wage policy was first introduced in Zhuhai (Guangdong) in 1989. From 52 yuan in 1989, it increased passed 235 yuan in 1995.

Theoretically, wage policy applies to all enterprises irrespective of the type of ownership, but local government and administrators may decide otherwise in cases where workers depend mainly on wage income for their livelihood. Minimum wage is referred to as the lowest remunerative due for the regular amount of labor provided during the legal work time.[141] Corresponding rules must be established by enterprises which follow a piece or a percentage wage system. This must be met irrespective of other kinds of wage incomes, including houses, housing and welfare benefits. Labor law reform by the turn of the 1990s was intended to create a strong labor market and consolidate the movement to market socialism.

The rude awakening of market socialism, the opening up of the Chinese market, and the labor law made the enterprises rather than the state decide on matters of employment and wages. By so doing the state abdicated from its original commitment and left workers at the mercy of the enterprises. The failed proletarian state enabled several enterprises to recklessly hire workers on contracts which are bogus. In Shantou and Zhuhai, for instance, only 30 and 10 percent (respectively) of labor contracts are valid. Enterprises dismiss workers at will, with little or no legal remedy, for the workers.[142] A survey of 217 foreign-funded enterprises in Guangdong province in 1996 shows that in the majority of plants the working day lasts 10 to 12 hours, sometimes 14, and there are instances of employees working for 28 hours without interruption.[143] Overtime with no benefits or remuneration is made compulsory in some enterprises. In this pusillanimous state, embezzlement and elopement are evident practices in the exploitation of workers.

These disputes are projecting increased role for the Chinese courts as the state backs down. The new labor law prescribes that from a mediation committee through an arbitration committee of local governments, disputes can now get to the courts as a last resort. Whether the courts will be efficacious is clearly unknown.

Labor disputes are rising fast not only in foreign, but state and urban collective enterprises. Though wages went up by the start of the 1990s, 33.6 percent of disputes involved wages and insurance issues. The impetus to strikes heightened, as workers applied for authorization to stage demonstrations. A survey of 10 provinces in 1994, shows that the number of major incidents in the second quarter of 1993 was 83.9 percent above that in the same period in 1992.[144] There has obviously been a breakdown of economic justice, and the gap between rich and poor has widened.

Within the same job categories there are variations in pay, between 900 and 5000 yuan for secretaries, and between $900 and U.S. $1200 for professionals. Gender discrimination makes it possible for women to earn 50 percent less than their male counterparts, even if the latter are less competent.[145] Bad income distribution, ill-gotten wealth, and defalcation of public funds are all prerequisites for political and economic instability.

Contemporary China shows that labor conflicts defy simple solutions, and the state as a concept carries with it many responsibilities in the global economy. The proletarian state and market socialism form a bewildering oxymoron from which economic justice is yet to be achieved.

The acquisition of equilibrium in all societies cannot be obtained by laws and their interpretations or enforcement, but by a reciprocal modification of demands. This is what positive law cannot legislate or achieve. That man has not been able to achieve economic justice, and is still looking out for it, is one major indication that positive law cannot tame the wild and innate proclivities of man to be greedy and acquisitive. Positive law has barely concocted a sense of justice to sedate those riotous instincts in man, so that in economic relations stability will be achieved for the continued creation of wealth. The overturn of economic injustice by positive law is utopian, but the disproportionate distribution of returns can be minimized under great difficulties. This is so because distribution of returns has effects on productive capacity, and therefore the reproduction of wealth. No human system can be made comprehensive enough to ignore this reality and replace it with a system of total economic justice in the economic relations of production.

Concluding Remarks

Conflict management in China, using the state clearly proved to be a failure. It is not too easy to understand the direction in which Mao was going because of the contradictions which attended his policies at various points in time. I have stayed clear off these contradictions because they do not fit into my fundamental arguments.

My selection of the proletarian state is based on the basic arguments that go with any socialist regime—the idea of emphasizing the state and workers for a transition to communism, which was affirmed by the part congress of June 1945. Mao started off with the proletarianization of the peasantry which conforms with a Marxist preoccupation with urban-rural conflicts. As a matter of initial policy, he constituted communism under the theory that workers will be united and represented by the proletarian communist party.

What happened in China was an attempt by Mao to use state power to impose his own ideas about a sense of economic justice on millions of Chinese by appealing to selective versions of Marxism. Confiscations and land redistribution were integral to his sense of justice, but by alienating private capital and modernization, he challenged basic precepts of Marxism that were vital to preparing China for the enhancement of general welfare. His understanding of the problems in economic relations was correct but his diagnosis was seriously flawed. This probably left him a confused man with contradictory policies, which did not really salvage the problem of the Chinese workers. He desperately wanted the Chinese to make a great leap, but in the process, all the indignities of labor that a working class revolution will seek to debunk descended on the Chinese workers—long hours of work, meager pay, and even slave labor.

The collapse of the classical proletarian state left a bewildering legacy, that necessitated the need for reform and the advent of market socialism. By relinquishing the primary role in conflict management, the state has left workers still groping for what they believe is achievable—-maximum economic justice. This expectation is still too ambitious. One major issue here is the extent to which socialism can be reformed to ascertain legal rights in a situation where the state prevails.

The reformers distanced themselves from basic Maoist policies, because of a lack of confidence in such policies which brought hardship and created conditions for China to struggle in order to gain adequate recognition in the global economy. There could be no gainsaying that trade increases economic welfare of any state, and that the more intrusive a state becomes the greater the potential for misdiagnosis.

Notes

Chapter 1. The Roman Slaves

1. Slaves were so-called because they were captives of war who had been spared by Roman commanders.

2. The monarchy came to an end in 509 B.C. after the expulsion of Tarquinius Superbus and ushered in the Roman Republic.

3. The origin of this categorization is obscure, but it is normally held that the patricians formed the original citizen body. The underprivileged class, which was differentiated from the plebeians, included fugitive aliens or manumitted slaves. See Lee's *The Elements of Roman Law*, p. 34.

4. The law otherwise known as natural law, *jus naturale or jus civile*.

5. Opinions of the jurists which abound in the Justinian Institutes help to define the Roman law of slavery. By the time of Justinian codification, Roman law was divided into such categories as public law and private law. These categories have points of intersection. Public law is directly related to the constitution of the state. It consisted of administrative law, constitutional law and criminal law. Private law deals with the relations of citizens, one to another, for example,laws dealing with the family, property, obligations and succession. Private law is believed to have come from principles of natural law, based on cherished traditions.

6. *Veteres*, meaning ancients.

7. For approximately a century after the enactment of the *Twelve Tables*, the interpretation of the law and of actions founded upon it was handled by the College of Pontiffs. Some of the greatest drawbacks in Roman legal history are attributed to this period of great contrivances and perversion.

8. Quoted in *The Elements of Roman Law*, p. 7.

9. Lee, op. cit., p. 8.

10. See Watson's *Slave Law In the Americas*, p. 4.

11. Praetors could give interdicts that are binding. For example, *exhibeas* (to produce), *restituas* (to resolve), and *veto* (to prohibit).

12. The *sella curulis* was a special chair of state. The aediles who were honored to sit on the chair were referred to as *curule aediles*.

13. They were so-called because they lived outside the Roman Empire, and were not assimilated into Roman culture. Current usage of the term is probably related to this lack of perceived civility, but equally so the havoc and destruction that was wreaked on the Western Roman Empire by the Barbarian invasion. Also, see Lee, op. cit., p. 21.

14. The *Institutes* included the work of ancient jurists whom the emperors gave authority to write and interpret the laws. Most important clarifications form its basis.

15. Quoted in Watson, *Roman Slave Law*, p. 49.

16. See Watson, 1987, p. 98; and Phillips, *American Negro Slavery*, p. 17.

17. The usufructuary rule made the rewards for slave labor from a third party beneficial to the master, since the master was the facilitator of the performance of labor.

18. Gai. *Instit.* 2:87, 89, p. 91-95.

19. The *Justinian Digest* gives some exceptions to adultery, theft, and self-defense. According to praetorian edict, when a slave is put to torture without his master's authority, the call for inquiry will be appropriate.

20. Gai. *Instit.* 2:88.

21. Lee, op. cit., p. 298.

22. See also Justinian, *Novel,* p. 78.

23. Gai. *Instit.* 17.

24. *Jus Conubi,* gave the husband a right to contract a civil law marriage with the wife. In the earliest Roman times, there was a conubium between Romans and Latins (inhabitants of the colonies). Children then followed the status of their fathers. See also Gai. *Institit.* 1:78.

Chapter 2. The Serfs

25. The kingdoms which replaced the disrupted Carolingian Empire are referred to as feudal. In them we see a merger of Roman and Germanic culture, which formed a new composite differing from the old and what we classify as modern.

26. The *Libri Feudorum* was a collection of technical literature defining "the good customs of the courts" in eleventh century Italy. See Bloch *Feudal Society,* p. 178

27. Loc. cit.

28. Spelman is an English legal historian. One of his writings include *The Archaeologus,* 1626.

29. Feudalism in English law is defined to mean a piece of land held in tenure which the courts recognize as heritable depending on approved or cognizable fixed rules. See Pocock, p. 65.

30. See Pocock's, *Ancient Constitution and the Feudal Law,* p. 71.

31. See Gukovsky, *The History of Feudalism,* p. 8.

32. See Ferguson and Brunn, op. cit., p. 103.

33. See Todd, *Everyday Life of the Barbarians,* p. 26

34. The term *Norman* or *Nartmanni* (Northmen) was used generally in Western Europe to describe the Barbarian heathen pirates. They were notorious for their destructive capabilities, but were forced to come to terms with the Carolingian and Capetian dynasties. Most eventually adopted Christianity as a religion and French as a language. They grasped the principles of Carolingian feudalism, and Normandy became in the eleventh century one of the most highly Feudalized states in Western Europe.

35. See Ganshof, *Feudalism,* p. 34.

36. *Commendatio* is the legal term also known as *munderburdis* or *patrocinium.* See Ganshof, op. cit., p. 6.

37. Calling the fief a piece of land only is misleading (Stephenson), for bare acres would have marginal value to the professional warrior, who considered the work of agriculture degrading.In law the fief could be indivisible, affirming that in some senses it was a public office rather than a mere piece of land. There seems to be some confusion over its usage. It seems to me, however, that public office and ownership of land must have gone *in tandem*.

38. See Bloch, op. cit., p. 373.

39. See Seignobos, *The Feudal Regime*, p. 25. *Justitia* was a lucrative property.

40. See Gukovsky, op. cit., P. 5.

41. Some significant revolts occurred in Normandy (1100). The Wat Tyler's Rebellion (1381) was the first great popular rebellion in English history attributed to a poll tax.

Chapter 3. The American Slaves

42. Quoted in Nettles, *The Roots of American Civilization*, p. 108. In 1583, Gilbert was lost at sea and his rights to America passed to his half-brother, Sir Walter Raleigh, who received his own patent in 1584, but was charged with treason and convicted in 1603. The men to whom he granted concessions, organized a new colonizing venture, and in 1606 obtained a Charter from James I.

43. For a comprehensive analysis of the Somerset case, see Hollander *Slavery In America*, p. 1-15.

44. See Philips *American Negro Slavery*, p. 489.

45. Quoted in Finkleman *The Law of Freedom and Bondage*, p. 6. Reference is also made to A. M. Stroud's, *A Sketch of the Laws Relating To Slavery In the Several States of the U.S.*

46. Cited in Hollander *Slavery In America*, p. 15.

47. See Peabody "Race Slavery, and the Law in Early Modern France" *The Historian*, p. 503.

48. For a more detailed survey of slavery law in Spain and Spanish America, see Watson *Slave Law in the Americas*, pp. 40-62.

49. See Kolchin *American Slavery* 1619-1877, p. 28.

50. Hollander, op. cit., p. 16.

51. See Nettles, op. cit., p. 132. The practice probably went back to the ninth century during the time of King Alfred.

52. Ibid.

53. See Finkelman, op. cit., p.1.

54. See Goodell *American Slave Code*, p. 264.

55. See Wheeler *Law of Slavery*, pp 340- 346. The ruling tends to have been influenced by Mansfield's proclamation.

56. See Wheeler, op. cit., p. 15.

57. This means article of personal property not attached to land. Immovable, because they are real rather than personal.

58. Goodell, op. cit., p. 25.

59. Goodell, op. cit., p. 28.

60. Whipping was legally thought to be a rather less severe punishment by owners of slaves.

61. See Goodell, op. cit., p. 169.

62. Cited in Goodell, p. 94.

63. For a detailed information about the 1850 Act, see the Fugitive Slave Bill of 1850.

64. In Prigg v. Pennsylvania, the slave owner himself was given authority to arrest an alleged fugitive without warrant from a magistrate.

65. This was legitimized by some state legislatures, including the Louisiana (1819).

66. Quoted in Goodell, op. cit., p. 232.

67. Cited in Goodell, op. cit., p. 236.

68. See Goodell, op. cit., p. 248.

69. See Wheeler *Law of Slavery*, p. 2.

70. Goodell, op. cit., p. 91.

71. See Wheeler *Law of Slavery*, p. 441.

Chapter 4. The American Workers

72. See Nevins and Commagner *A Pocket History of the United States*, p. 256.

73. The Statute of Artificers (1562-63) was a reenactment in a modified form of all the main features of earlier Statutes of Laborers. According to the Statute of Laborers, oral employment agreements were enforceable in common law in thirteenth century England. The Statute of Artificers laid provisions whereby, through writs of Capias, a master could recover runaway servants. Justices issued writs, and the sheriff could incarcerate apprehended runaways until the court was sure that they could serve their master faithfully. For further survey, see Holdsworth, W.S., p. 460, vol. 2; Steinfeld, R.J., p.22. Putnam, B.H., parts 1 and 2 chap. 2; and Orren, K., "Labor Regulation And Constitutional Theory In The United States And England," *Political Theory*, Feb. 1994, p. 101; also Orren, K., *Belated Feudalism*, p. 100.

74. Steinfeld, R., *The Invention of Free Labor*, p. 17.

75. Orren *Belated Feudalism*, p. 74.

76. Nevins and Commager, op. cit., p. 283.

77. I have used 1842 as a cut off point, because the Hunt case was intended to undo charges of conspiracy.

78. The New York and Pennsylvania legislatures passed four each. See *American Business Law Journal*, vol. 32, 1994, p. 139.

79. Orren, K. op. cit., p. 81.

80. Orren, K. *Political Theory*, Feb. 1995, p. 108.

81. In this case boot makers were convicted of conspiracy for using the economic pressure of a strike to obtain a closed shop (the hiring of employees who are members of good standing in unions). Chief Justice Lemuel

Shaw of the Massachusetts Supreme Court overturned the lower courts conviction of the workers, holding that they should be free to organize for collective action. See *American Business Law Journal*, 1994, vol. 32, p. 129. See also Leslie, D. L., *Labor Law*, p.1., and Myers, A. H., *Labor Law and Legislation*, p. 17.

82. Even after the late 1870s, people were charged with labor conspiracies on many occasions. Some Molly Maguire members, for example, were hanged between 1877 and 1879 after being charged with conspiracy to commit murder. The Molly Maguires, also known as *Bukshots, White Boys,* and *Sleepers* took their name from a widow called Molly Maguire, who led a group of anti-landlord agitators in the 1840s. Members of the group were predominantly of Irish origin. The members murdered or intimidated recalcitrant mine bosses and colliery superintendents. See *Dictionary of American History*, vol. 4., 1976, p. 391; Levy and Richard *Struggle and Lose, Struggle and Win*, p. 21 and Bergamin, *The Hundredth Year: The U.S. in 1876*, p. 33. The Maguires were an outgrowth of a fraternal organization of an ancient order of Hibernians. Whenever the price of labor fell, they would organize a strike.

83. Noble was added to its name after the election of Terrence Powderly in 1879.

84. The Act derived its name from John Sherman, a senator from Ohio, who was one of its leading architects. Many of the supportive senators, like Edmonds of Vermont, Hoar of Massachusetts and George of Mississippi, saw it as an affirmation of an old common law doctrine. Contrary to expectations, it became a coup de grace that really challenged attempts at unionization and aided an era of injunctions that strengthened the basis for voluntarism, a nongovernmental solution to labor-management problems.

85. See Forbath *Law and the Shaping of American Labor Movement*, p. 62. By conservative reckoning between 1880 and 1930, forty-three hundred injunctions were issued.

86. Forbath, op. cit., p. 71.

87. See Frankfurter and Greene, *The Labor Injunction*, p. 6; Myers, *Labor Law and Legislation*, p. 177, and Cox and Bok, *Labor Law*, p. 63.

88. See Frankfurter and Greene, op. cit. p. 8.

89. See the Gompers v. Bucks Stove and Range Co., 221 US 418 (1911). For related cases see also Frankfurter and Greene, op. cit. p. 5-46.

90. Quoted in Myers, op. cit. p. 76. See also Leslie, *Labor Law*, p. 3.

91. Forbath, op.cit., p. 75.

92. Forbath, op. cit., p. 68.

93. The Commission was set up to investigate the causes of the Pullman Strike.

94. See *Congressional Digest*, June-July 1993, p. 164. After two amendments (1936 and 1950), this Act became known as the Celler- Kefauver Act.

95. See Wellington, op. cit., p. 39.

96. Yellow-dog contracts are contracts in which employees either promise not to join unions, or quit the membership of unions to which they are already attached. This was used largely in the 1920s to enable employers to take legal actions against union organizers for encouraging workers to break the contracts. In Adair v. US (1908), the Supreme Court held such contracts as constitutionally guaranteeing freedom of contract. A federal law prohibiting the use of yellow-dogs on the railroads was struck down (Erdman Act 1898). See *Congressional Digest*, June-July 1993, p. 163. The injunctions were intended to uphold the yellow-dogs.

97. The President originally appointed three members.

98. Closed shop and Union shop requires in the first instance that an employer hires only union members in good standing, and in the second, that an employee joins a union to keep his or her job.

99. See *Congressional Digest*, June-July 1993, p. 165.

100. Friedman, et. al. *Restoring the Promise of American Labor Law*, p. 15.

101. For detailed information, see *Congressional Digest*, June-July 1993, p. 166.

102. Loc. cit.

103. Friedman, et. al. op. cit., p. 46

104. See New Negro Alliance v. Sanitary Grocery Co. Inc. (1938); Milk Wagon Drivers' Union v. Lake Valley; Brotherhood of Railroad Trainmen v. Chicago & Ind. Railroad Co. (1957), and Sinclair Refining Co. v. Akinson.

105. Mackay Radio and Telegraph Co. v. NLRB (1938). Quoted in Leslie, op. cit., p. 96.

106. See Friedman et. al. op. cit., p. 61-74.

107. See *National Law Journal*, Nov. 29, 1993, vol. 16, no. 13, p. 514.

Chapter 5. The British Workers

108. See Cole's *A History of the British Working Class Movement*, 1789-1947, p. 4.

109. This law made provision for reprisals should a breach of contract occur. Examples of a breach include premature departure from work or work stoppage.

110. Cole, op. cit., p. 40.

111. By the Statute of Artificers, workers normally were bonded to work with a master for a particular period of time.

112. The introduction of Universal Suffrage in the late 1880s was relevant to the interest of workers. Until this period, property qualification was a necessary precondition for election to Parliament.

113. Cole cites some of the outcomes of the repeal: The Steam Engine Makers' Society and London Shipwrights' Association (1824); Northumberland and Durham Colliers (1825); the Journeymen Steam Engine Makers (1826); and the General Union of Carpenters and Joiners (1827).

114. Cole, op.cit., p. 171.

115. During the general lockout, employers withheld work from employees and closed down a plant during labor disputes.

116. Quoted in Cleg et.al. *A History of British Trade Unions Since 1889* p. 44; and Cole, op.cit., p. 201. An Amalgamated Society of Engineers (ASE) originally was formed in 1826 to subvert subcontracting ventures that benefited employers; it was remodeled in the 1880s. One of its major objectives was to protect its funds against defalcations and defaulting officials. As a matter, of fact the success of trade unions is strongly dependent on financial strength.

117. The *voluntarist* solution entails negotiation between workers and employers without external intervention.

118. These laws made picketing legal, repealed the Criminal Act of 1871, and gave trade unions a great deal of adequate legal status and immunity in the conduct of industrial disputes. Generally, though, the laws withheld from trade unions the rights and responsibilities of incorporation.

119. This was implied in provisions of section 4 of the Trade Union Act of 1871.

120. Quoted in Cleg et. al. vol. 1, op.cit., p. 291; Fulcher, *Labour Movement Employers and the State*, p. 85; and Minkin, *The Contentious Alliance: Trade Unions and the Labour Party*, p. 11.

121. See Taff Vale case in *Encyclopedia Britannica, Micropaedia*, vol. 11, 1990.

122. See Cleg, *A History of British Trade Unions Since 1889*, vol. 2, p. 362.

123. For a detailed discussion of the issues, see Michael Klarman "Parliamentary Reversal of the Osborne Judgement," *The Historical Journal*, vol. 32, no. 4, 1989, p. 893-924.

124. See Alderman, K. and Carter, "The Labour Party and the Trade Unions: Loosening the Ties,"*Parliamentary Affairs*, July 1994, vol. 47, no. 3, p. 321-337.

125. See *The Economist*, Sept. 9-15, 1995, p. 62.

Chapter 6. The Chinese Workers

126. Mao's communist revolution is considered a proletarian revolution by the seventh National Party Congress of the Communist Party of China on June 11, 1945.

127. See *Labor Problems In Communist China*, Human Resources Research Institute, Sept., 1955. p. 1.

128. Loc. cit.

129. The Bureau of Labor was charged with the responsibility of conciliating and arbitrating labor disputes in public and private enterprises.

130. See "Collective v. Individual Rights," *Beijing Review*, Sept. 15, 1994, p. 3.

131. See "The Trade Union Law of the People's Republic of China," adopted by the GAC on June 28, 1950, *People's China* supplement to vol. 11, no. 2, July 16, 1950, p. 8-11.

132. See also *The Chinese World*, July 10, 1952.

133. See *Labor Problems in Communist China*, op. cit., p. 37.

134. Grenville, *A History of the World in the Twentieth Century*, p. 634.

135. "Wages: After the Labor Law," *China News Analysis*, Oct. 1, 1995.

136. "Shangai Changes in Ownership Structure," *Beijing Review*, Mar. 28-April 3, 1994.

137. Przeworski, *Democracy and the Market*, p. 124-125.

138. "China's Economic Reform and Opening," Beijing Review, Jan. 8-14, 1996, p. 16.

139. Grenville, op. cit., p. 649.

140. "The Minimum Wage Policy," *China News Analysis*, Oct. 1, 1995, p. 2.

141. Loc. cit.

142. "A Labor Law?" *China News Analysis*, Jan. 15, 1994, p. 2.

143. Loc. cit. See also "Unions Urged In Foreign-Funded Firms," *Beijing Review*, June 3-9, 1996.

144. Wages went up in 1994 and 1995. In 1994 total wages reached 665 billion yuan, which is about 35.3 percentage points over 1993. This is about the highest in 16 years. See *China News Analysis*, Oct. 1, 1995, p. 8; and Jan. 15, 1994.

145. "Wages: After the Labor Law," *China News Analysis*, Oct. 1, 1995, p. 9.

Bibliography

Aaron, B. and K.W. Wedderburn. eds. *Industrial Conflict: A Comparative Legal Survey.* New York: Crane, Russak and Company, 1973.

Abrahamsson, Bengt. *The Rights of Labor.* Beverly Hills, CA: Sage Publications, California, 1980.

Alderman, K. "The Labour Party and the Trade Unions," *Parliamentary Affairs* 47.3 (1994): 321-37.

Anderson, P. "Breaking Up Is Hard to Do," *New Statesman and Society* 8.352 (1995): 14.

Ansden, J. and S. Brier. "Coal Miners on Strike: The Transformation of Strike Demands and the Formation of a National Union." *Journal of Interdisciplinary History,* Spring 1977.

Astarita, Tommaso. *The Continuity of Feudal Power.* Cambridge, NY: Cambridge University Press, 1992.

Aurand, H. *From the Molly Maguires to the United Mine Workers: The Social Ecology of an Industrial Union.* Philadelphia: Temple University Press, 1971.

Avineri, S. *Social and Political Thought of Karl Marx.* New York: Cambridge University Press, 1971.

Baldwin, Roger Nash. *A New Slavery, Forced Labor: The Communist- Betrayal of Human Rights.* New York: Oceana Publication, 1953.

Balinky, A. *Marx's Economics: Origin and Development.* Indianapolis: D.C. Heath and Company, 1970.

Ballam, D.A. "The Law As a Constitutive Force for Change." *American Business Law Journal* 32, No. 1 (1994): 125-49.

Ballot, M. "British Labor Relations and the Law," *Labor Law Journal* 47.4 (1996): 250-520.

Barnett, A. D. *China After Mao.* New Jersey: Princeton University Press, 1967.

Bauman, Z. *Socialism: The Active Utopia.* New York: Holmes and Meier Publishers, Inc.,1976.

Baxter, S. "Strikes?" *New Statesman and Society* 6.245 (1993): 22.

Beal, E.F. and J.P. Begin. *The Practice of Collective Bargaining.* Homewood, IL: Richard D. Irwin, 1982.

Bergamini, J.D. *The Hundredth Year: The United States in 1876.* New York: G.P. Putnam's Sons, 1976.

Bianco, L. *Origins of the Chinese Revolution 1915-1944.* London: Oxford University Press, 1971.

Bloch, M. *Feudal Society.* Chicago: Chicago University Press, Chicago, 1961.

Blum, A. A. *International Handbook Of Industrial Relations: Contemporary Developments and Research.* Westport, CT: Greenwood Press, 1981.

Boroff, K.E. "Law and the Shaping of American Labor Movement," *Journal of Labor Research* 14, No. 1 (1993): 95.

Boyer, Richard O. and Herbert M. Morais. *Labor's Untold Story.* New York: United Electrical, Radio, and Machine Workers of America, 1973.

Bradley, K.R. *Slavery and Rebellion in the Roman World 140-70 B.C.* Bloomington: Indiana University Press, 1989.

Braun, Kurt. *Labor Disputes and Their Settlement.* Baltimore: Johns Hopkins Press, 1955.

Brecher, Jeremy. *Strike.* Greenwich, CT: Fawcett Publishers, 1974.

Brooks, T.R. *Toil and Trouble: A History of American Labor.* New York: Delacorte Press, 1971.

Brown, K.D. *Essays in Anti-Labour History.* Great Britain: The Macmillan Press, 1974.

Brown, S. M. "Inalienable Rights," in *Contemporary Political Theory*, ed. A. Decrespingy and Wertheimer. New York: Atherton Press, 1970.

Buckland, W.W. *The Roman Law of Slavery.* Cambridge: Cambridge University Press, 1908.

Burns, E.M. and Ralph, P.L. *World Civilizations.* New York: W.W. Norton, 1974.

Cahn, W.A. *A Pictorial History of American Labor.* New York: Crown Publishers, Inc., 1972.

Cary, M. and H.H. Scullard, *A History of Rome Down to the Reign of Constantine.* New York: St. Martin's Press, 1975.

Catlin, W.B. *The Labor Problem in the U.S. and Great Britain.* New York: Harper and Brothers, 1935.

Ch'en, S. *Mao's Betrayal.* Moscow: Progress, 1975.

Chamberlain, N.W. and Cullen, D.E. *The Labor Sector*. New York: McGraw-Hill Book Company, 1971.

Chambre, H. *From Karl Marx to Mao Tse-tung*. New York: Kennedy, 1963.

Clarkson, L.A. *British Trade Union and Labour History*. New Jersey: Humanities Press International, Inc., 1988.

Cleg, H.A. *A History of British Trade Unions Since 1889: 1911-1933*. Vol. 2. New York: Oxford University Press, 1985.

Clubb, O.E. *20th Century China*. New York: Columbia University Press, 1964.

Cole, G.D.H. *A Short History of the British Working Class Movement 1789-1947*. Great Britain: University of Aberdeen Press, 1948.

Cole, J. "The Way to Voters' Hearts," *New Statesman and Society* 15.202 (1992): 9.

Cooper, J.M. "Army as Strikebreaker in the Railroad Strikes of 1877 and 1894," *Labor History*, spring 1977, 18 2:179-96.

Cox, A. and D.C. Bok, *Labor Law*. New York: The Foundation Press, 1965.

Craig, M., et. al. *The Heritage of World Civilizations*. Vol. 1. Macmillan Publishing Company, New York, 1990.

Curtis, M. *Marxism*. New York: Atherton Press, 1970.

DeTocqueville, A. *Democracy in America*. Trans. by J.P. Mayer. Garden City: Doubleday & Co., Inc., 1969.

Dickins, A. "Divided We Stand," *New Statesman and Society* 7:284 (1994): 1.

Dictionary of American History. Vol. 4. New York: Charles Scribner's Sons, 1976.

Dorfman, G.A. *Government Versus Trade Unionism in British Polltics Since 1968.* Great Britain: Macmillan Press Ltd., 1979.

Dubofsky, M. *Industrialism and the American Worker*: 1865-1920. Arlington Heights, IL. Ahm Publishing Corp., 1975.

Dunlop, J.T. and Galenson, W. eds., *Labor in the Twentieth Century.* New York: Academic Press, 1978.

Eatwell, J., et al. *A Dictionary of Economics.* London: The Macmillan Press Ltd., 1987.

Elv, R.T. *The Labor Movement in America.* New York: J.Y. Crowell and Co., 1886.

Estey, M. *The Unions.* New York: Harcourt, Brace, Jovanovich, 1981.

Feather, Victor. *The Essence of Trade Unionism.* Chester Springs, PA, 1963

"Federal Labor Laws," *Congressional Digest* 72, No.6-7 (1993): 164- 66.

Ferguson, W. and G. Bruun. *A Survey of European Civilization.* 1962.

Fetscher, I. *Marx and Marxism.* New York: Herder and Herder, 1971.

Finkelman, Paul. *The Law of Freedom and Bondage*. Dobbs Ferry: Oceana Publications, NY, 1986.

Fischer, E. *Essential Marx*. New York: Herder and Herer, 1970.

Fleisher, B. M. and T.J. Kniesner. *Labor Economics: Theory, Evidence, and Policy*. Englewood Cliffs, NJ: Prentice Hall, 1970.

Foner, P. *The Great Labor Uprising of 1877*. New York: Monad Press, 1978.

Forbath, W.E. *Law and the Shaping of the American Labor Movement*. Boston: Harvard University Press, 1991.

Foriers, P. and C. Perelman. "Natural Law and Natural Rights," *Dictionary of the History of Ideas*. New York: Charles Scribner's Sons, 1973.

Frankfurter, Felix and N. Green. *The Labor Injunction*. New York: Macmillan, 1930.

Friedman, S., et al. *Restoring the Promise of American Labor Law*. New York: ILR Press, 1994.

Frier, B.W. "Roman Slave Law," *American Historical Review* 93.4 (1988): 1026.

Fulcher, J. *Labour Movements Employers and the State*. New York: Oxford University Press, 1991.

Fusfeld, D. R., *The Age of Economist*. New York: Harper Collins Publishers, 1990.

Gall, P. and J. Hoen. "Growing Schism Between Business and Labor," *Business Week*, 14 Aug. 1978, p. 78.

Ganshof, F.L. *Feudalism*. Great Britain: Northampton: John Dicken & Co., Ltd., 1964.

Gelb, N. "Tony Blair's Strategy," *New Leader* 77.8 (1994): 3.

Goldberg, J.P. "The Law and Practice of Collective Bargaining." *Federal Policies and Worker Status Since the Thirties.* Madison, WI: Industrial Relations Research Associates, 1976.

Goodell, W. *The American Slave Code*. New York: Negro University Press, 1968.

Gordon, W.M. and O.F. Robinson. *The Institutes of Gaius*. New York: Cornell University Press, 1988.

Gregory, C.O. *Labour and the Law*. New York: W.W. Norton, 1946.

Grenville, J.A.S. *A History of the World in the Twentieth Century*. Boston: Harvard University Press, 1994.

Grundel, J. "Natural Law." *Encyclopedia of Theology: The Concise Sacramentum Mundi*. Ed. K. Rahner. New York: The Seabury Press, 1975.

Gukovsky, A.I. *History of Feudalism*. Moscow: State Textbook Publishing House, 1935.

Harrington, M. *Socialism*. New York: Saturday Review Press, 1972.

Haskins, J. *The Long Struggle: The Story of American Labor*. Philadelphia: Westminster Press, 1976.

Hawkins, K.H. *Trade Unions*. London: Hutchinson Publishing Group Ltd., 1981.

Heilbroner, R.L. "What Is Socialism?" *Dissent*. Summer, 1978.

Helfand, B.F. "Labor and the Courts: The Common-Law Doctrine of Criminal Conspiracy and Its Application in the Buck's Stove Case," *Labor History*, Spring 1977, 18: 2: 91-114.

Herndon, D. "Redefining the Boundaries of Labor Protest After Madsen v. Women's Health Center," *Labor Law Journal*. January, 47. no.1 (1996): 32-53.

Hildebrand, G. H. *American Unionism: An Historical and Analytical Survey*. Reading, MA: Addison-Wesley Publishing Company, Inc., 1979.

Holdsworth, William Searle, Sir. *A History of English Law*. Boston: Little Brown, 1922.

Hollander, B. *Slavery in America*. New York: Barnes and Noble, Inc., 1963.

Hollander, S. *The Economics of Adam Smith*. Buffalo: University of Toronto Press, 1973.

Holmes, M. *The Labour Government 1974-1979*. London: Macmillan and Co., 1985.

Horne, J. "Capitalism and Unfree Labour," *Sociological Review* 37.3 (1989): 562-66.

Howe, Stephen. "Unblocking Labour," *New Statesman and Society* 1.3 (1988): 21.

Hudson, J. *Land Law and Lordship in Anglo-Norman England*. Oxford: Oxford University Press, 1994.

Hughes, J. *American Economic History*. Glenview, Illinois: Scott Foresman and Company, 1983.

Jevons, W.S. *The State in Relation to Labour*. London: Macmillan and Co., 1894.

Joel, K. *The Oxford Companion to Politics of the World*. New York: Oxford University Press, 1993.

Jolowicz, H.F. and B. Nicholas *Historical Introduction to the Study of Roman Law*. Cambridge: Cambridge University Press, 1972.

"Judicial decision in the field of Labor Law," *International Law Review* 132, No. 2 (1993): 209-301.

Kauper, P. G. "The Higher Law and the Rights of Man In a Revolutionary Society." *America's Continuing Revolution*. Ed. Irving

Kidner, R. *Trade Unions*. London: Sweet and Maxwell, 1980.

Klarman, M.J. "Parliamentary Reversal of the Osborne Judgement," *Historical Journal* 32, No. 4 (1989): 893-924.

Knight, F.W. "Slave Law in the Americas," *Hispanic American Historical Review* 71 (1991): 389.

Kolchin, Peter. *American Slavery 1619-1877*. New York: Whill and Wang, 1993.

Kovach, K. A. *Readings and Cases In Contemporary Labor Relations*. Washington, D.C.: University Press Of America, 1981.

Kreps, J.M., et al. *Contemporary Labor Economics and Labor Relations.* Belmont, CA: Wadsworth Publishing Company, 1980.

Krieger, J., et. al. *The Oxford Companion to Politics of the World.* New York: Oxford University Press, 1993.

Kristol, et.al., Washington, D.C.: American Enterprise Institute, 1975.

Kuhn, W.E. *The Evolution of Economic Thought.* Cincinnati: South-western Publishing Company, 1970.

"Labor, Regulation, and Constitutional Theory in the U.S. and England," *Political Theory* 22, no. 1 (1994) 98-123.

"Labor-Management Bargaining in 1995" *Monthly Labor Review.* 119.1,2 (1996): 25-46.

"Labour Pains," *Spectator* 271, No.8618 (1993): 5.

"Labour Law: Kicking the Corpse," *The Economist.* 320, No. 7717 (1991): 56.

"Labour and the Unions," *The Economist* 336.7931 (1995): 62.

Lanqing, L. "China's Economic Reform and Opening," *Beijing Review* Jan.8-14, 1996.

Lee, R.W. *The Elements of Roman Law.* London: Sweet and Maxwell Ltd., 1956.

Lens, S. *The Labor Wars, from the Molly Maguires to the Sitdowns.* Garden City: Doubleday and Co., 1973.

Leslie, D.L. *Labor Law.* St. Paul, MN: West Publishing Company, 1992.

Letwin, S. R. "Modern Philosophies of Law." *The Great Ideas Today.* Chicago: Encyclopedia Britannica, 1972.

Levy, E. and T. Richards. *Struggle and Lose, Struggle and Win: The United Mine Workers.* New York: Four Winds Press, 1977.

Lewis, Minkin. *The Contentious Alliance.* Edinburgh: Edinburgh University Press, 1991.

Lichtheim, G. "What Socialism Is and Is Not," *New York Review of Books* 9 April, 1976.

Lovenduski, J. "Labour and the Unions," *Government and Opposition* 29, No. 2 (1994): 201-17.

Mann, Nyta "Blair Reiterates Retreat from Unions," *New Statesman and Society* 7, No. 330 (1994): 9.

Marske, C., et al. "The Significance of Natural Law in Contemporary Legal Thought," *Catholic Lawyer*, Winter 1978.

Marx, K. and F. Engels. *The Communist Manifesto.* New York: Bantam Books, 1992.

McCulloch, F. W. and T. Bornstein. *The National Labor Relations Board.* New York: Praeger Publishers, 1974.

Mcfeely, W.S. "Were These People Property?" *New York Times Book Review.* Jan. 18, 1987 p. 9.

McGuiness, Jeffrey C. "Outdated Laws Govern Modern Workplaces," *National Law Journal* 16, No. 13 (1993): 514-15.

McKitterick, R. *The Frankish Kingdoms Under the Carolingians 751- 987*. New York: Longman, 1983.

McPherson, C. B. *The Rise and Fall of Economic Justice*. Oxford: Oxford University Press, 1987.

Meisner, M.J., *Marxism, Maoism, And Utopianism*. U.S.: University of Wisconsin Press, 1982

Meltzer, M. *Bread and Roses: The Struggle of American Labor 1865-1915*. New York: Random House, 1973.

Merkel, M. *The Labor Union Handbook*. New York: Beaufort Books, 1983.

Mills, D. *Labor-Management Relations*. New York: McGraw-Hill Book Company, 1978.

Milonakis, D. "Prelude to the Genesis of Capitalism," *Science and Society* 57, no. 4 (1993-1994): 390-419.

Milsom, S.F.C. *The Legal Framework of English Feudalism*. Cambridge: Cambridge University Press, 1976.

"The Minimum Wage Debate," *The Economist* (1995) Vol. 336 No. 7931 p. 58.

Morgan, K. "British Politics," *Political Studies* 42, no. 3 (1994): 525.

Muschamp, D. "Rousseau and the General Will." *Political Thinkers*. Ed. D. Muschamp. New York: St. Martins Press, 1986.

Myers, A.H. *Labor Law and Legislation*. Cincinnati, OH: South- Western Publishing Co., 1968.

"Natural Law," *Lutheran Encyclopedia*. Lueker, E. St. Louis: Concordia Publishing House, 1975.

"Natural Right to Equal Freedom," *Mind*. LXXXIII (1974): p. 194-210.

Neale, A.D. and D.G. Goyder. *Antitrust Laws of the U.S.A.* New York: Cambridge University Press, 1981.

Nettles, C.P. *The Roots of American Civilization*. New York: Appleton-Century Crofts, 1938.

Nevins, A. and H.S. Commager. *A Pocket History of the United States*. New York: Washington Square Press, 1986.

"Trends in Collective Bargaining and Industrial Relations," *Labor Law Journal* 28.8 (1977): 532-538.

"Social Security: The Unemployed and Retired," *China News Analysis* 15 Jan.,1994.

"Unions Urged in Foreign-Funded Firms," *Beijing Review* June 3-9, 1996.

"China and Human Rights," *China News Analysis* 15 Sept., 1994.

"Wages: After the Labor Law," *China News Analysis* 1 Oct., 1995.

"Justice As Fairness," *The Economist* 243.6715 (1977): 68.

"*U.S. News And World Report*" 20 Mar.1978.

Labor Problems in Communist China (To Feb. 1953). U.S.A.: Human Resources Research Institute, 1995.

Labor Law and Practice in Great Britain. U.S.A.: Bureau Of Labor Statistics, 1972.

Ning, L. "Framework for a Socialist Legal System," *Beijing Review* May 13-19, 1996.

Nnoli, O. *Introduction to Politics*. Hong Kong: Longman Group Ltd., 1986.

The Northern Barbarians 100 B.C.-A.D. 300. London: Hutchinson, 1975.

Nurse, L. A. "Custom and Practice in Labor Relations in the United States: A Review of the Evidence," *Labor Law Journal*. 30.1 (1979): 38-48.

Orren, K. *Belated Feudalism*. Cambridge: Cambridge University Press, 1991.

Parekh, B., ed. *The Concept of Socialism*. New York: Holmes and Meier Publishers, Inc., 1975.

Paul, E. F. "On the Theory of the Social Contract Within the Natural Rights Traditions," *Personalist* Jan.1978.

Peabody, S. "Race, Slavery, and the Law in Early Modern France," *The Historian* 56.3 (19_): 501-10.

Petrie, A. *An Introduction to Roman History Literature and Antiques*. London: Oxford University Press, 1963.

Phillips, U.B. *American Negro Slavery*. Baton Rouge: State University Press, 1969.

Phillips, W.D. *Slavery from Roman Times to Early Transatlantic Trade*. Minneapolis: University of Minnesota Press, 1985.

Pocock, J.G.A. *Ancient Constitution and the Feudal Law*. Cambridge: Cambridge University Press, 1987.

Przeworski, A. *Democracy and the Market*. Cambridge: Cambridge University Press, 1991.

Rawls, J. *A Theory of Justice*. Boston: Harvard University Press, 1971.

Rawson, E. "The Rise of the Roman Jurists," *American Historical Review* 91.3 (1986): 638.

Reck, A. J. "Natural Law in American Revolutionary Thought," *Review Of Metaphysics*, 17.2 (1977): 686-714.

Rousseau, J. *The Social Contract*. Trans. M. Cranston. England: Penguin Books, 1968.

Rowan, R.L. *Readings in Labor Economics and Labor Relations*. Illinois: Richard Irwin, 1976.

Rubin, A.R. *War Law and Labour*. Oxford: Claredan Press, 1987.

Ryder, A. "The Continuity of Feudal Power," *English Historical Review* 110:435 (1995): 193.

Sangerman, H. "Employee Committees: Can They Survive Under the Taft-Hartley Act," *Labor Law Journal* Oct. 1973.

Schechter, R.A. "Labor Law," *National Law Journal* 17.33 (1995): B5-B6.

Schram, S.R. *The Thought of Mao Tse-Tung*. New York: Cambridge University Press, 1989.

Seignobos, C. *The Feudal Regime*. New York: Henry Holt and Company, 1929.

The Settlement of Industrial Disputes. Philadelphia: The Blaksten Company, 1944.

Sherman, P.J. "Bargaining Over the Terms and Conditions for Striker Replacements: Is the NLRB about to Change the Rules?" *Labor Law Journal*. 47.3 (1996): 178-82.

Sherman, R. *Antitrust Policies and Issues*. Reading, MS: Addison-Wesley Publishing Company, Inc., 1978.

Shklar, J. *Men and Citizens: A Study of Rousseau's Social Theory*. New York: Cambridge University Press, 1985.

"Shutting Up Shop," *New Statesman and Society*. 2, No. 81 (1989: 5.

Simpson, A.W.B.. *A History of the Land Law*. New York: Clarendon Press, 1986.

Sinnigen, W.G. and A.E.R. Boak. *A History of Rome to A.D. 565*. New York: Macmillan Company, 1977

Slave Law in the Americas. Athens: University of Georgia Press, 1989.

Sloane, A. A.and Witney, F. *Labor Relations*. Englewood Cliffs, NJ: Prentice-Hall Inc., 1977.

So, A.Y. *Social Change and Development*. USA: Sage Publications, Inc., 1990.

Spiegal, H.W. *The Growth of Economic Thought*. Englewood Cliffs,NJ: Prentice-Hall, Inc., 1971.

Starr, J. B., *Continuing the Revolution: The Political Thought of Mao*. Princeton, NJ: Princeton University Press, 1979.

Steiner, H. "Natural Right to the Means of Production," *Philosophical Quarterly* Jan. 1977.

Steinfeld, R.J. *The Invention of Free Labor*. Chapel Hill: University of North Carolina Press, 1991.

Stephenson, C. *Mediaeval Feudalism*. New York: Great Seal Books, 1942.

Svallfors, Stefan, "Labour Movements: Employers and the State," *Acta Sociologica* 36.2 (1993): 156-58.

Taylor, B.J. and F. Witney. *Labor Relations Law*. NJ: Prentice- Hall, Inc.,1975.

Taylor, K. *The Political Ideas of the Utopian Socialists*. Totowa, NJ: Biblio Distribution Centre, 1978.

"Thatcher Reins in Labor's Legal Rights." *Business Week*, 14 Dec., 1981 p. 25.

Thomas, J.A. *Textbook of Roman Law*. New York: El Sevier-North, 1976.

Thompson, E.A. *Romans and Barbarians*. Madison: University of Wisconsin Press, 1982.

Tierney, B., et al. *The Decline and Fall of the Roman Empire*. Westminster, MD: Random House, 1977.

Todd, M. *Everyday Life of the Barbarians*. New York: Dorset Press, 1977.

"Tony Blair's First Year." *The Economist.* (1995):53. Vol. 336. No. 7924 p. 53.

Tucker, R.C. *Marxian Revolutionary Idea.* New York: W.W. Norton and Company Inc., 1970.

Undy, R., et al. *Change in Trade Unions: The Development of U.K. Unions Since the 1960s.* London: Hutchinson Publishing Group Ltd., 1981.

Vincent, A. *Theories of the State.* Cambridge: Oxford: Blackwell Publishers and Cambridge University Press, 1993.

Wakeman, F. E. *History and Will: Philosophical Perspectives of Mao Tse-tung's Thought.* Berkeley: University of California, 1973.

Waldron, J. *Theories of Rights.* U.S.A.: Oxford University Press, 1995.

Walker, D. M. *The Oxford Companion to Law.* Oxford: Clarendon Press, 1980.

Wallbank, T., et al. *Civilization Past and Present.* England: Scott, Foresman, and Company, 1987.

Walters, R.G. *American Reformers 1815-1860.* New York: Hill and Wang, 1978.

Watson, A. *Roman Slave Law.* Baltimore: Johns Hopkins University Press, 1987.

Webster, D. *The Labour Party and the New Left.* Britain: Fabian Society, 1981.

Wedderburn, K.W. and Benjamin, Aaron. *Industrial Conflict.* New York: Crane Russak, 1972.

Wellington, H.H. *Labor and the Legal Process*. U.S.: The Colonial Press Inc., 1968.

Westermann, W.L. *The Slave Systems of Greek and Roman Antiquity*. Philadelphia: American Philosophical Society, 1955.

Wheeler, J.D. *A Practical Treatise on the Law of Slavery*. New York: Negro University Press, 1968.

Wiedemann, T. *Greek and Roman Slavery*. Baltimore: Johns Hopkins University Press, 1981.

Wilczynski, J. *The Economics of Socialism*. Edison, NJ: Allen and Unwin, Inc., 1977.

Wood, Anthony. *Nineteenth Century Britain 1815-1914*. London: Longman, 1972.

Wood, J. "The Narrators of Barbarian History A.D. 550-800," *Canadian Journal of History*. 24, no.1 (1989): 92.

Ye, L. "Shangai: Change in Ownership Structure," *Beijing Review* Mar.28-Apr.3, 1994

Yellowitz, Irwin. *Industralization and the American Labor Movement, 1850-1960*. Port Washington, NY: Kennikat Press, 1977.

Yongjiang, G. "China to Establish Free Trade System," *Beijing Review* March 11-17, 1996.